"The best is the water."
The Greek lyric poet Pindar
(522-446 BC)

Ulrich Timm

Creating Ponds, Brooks, and Pools

Water in the Garden

with the cooperation of Hannelore Timm

4880 Lower Valley Road, Atglen, PA 19310 USA

Page 1: Supine youth, a sculpture by Anton Beijsens, in the garden of Corrie and Joop Poley. Water in the garden invites one to sweet idleness.

Page 2: Water in the garden has many facets. Is it cold and mysterious? Not necessarily, as shown by this swimming pool in sunny Perth, Australia. Here the water is clear and refreshing in the heat. It is the mirror of heaven—and perhaps also of the garden owners' lifestyle.

Right: A refreshing contrast: a pool formed by angled walls in warm colors turns the split, scarcely worked granite block into a living spring (Chandler).

Contents

Fascination with Water 6
The History of Ponds and Brooks 6
Planning and Building With a Garden Architect 12

The Loveliest Ponds and Brooks **14**
Twenty-five Exemplary Gardens

Ponds for Swimming 88
Ten Exemplary Gardens

Swimming Pools 114

The Loveliest Garden Pools 122

Plans and Layouts 138
The Best is the Water 138
The Right Choice 138
Details and Designs 138
The Location 142
The Size 142
The Shape 142
Materials 144
The Pond Bottom 144
The Shore 146
The Substrata 146
The Water 146
Safety 146

The Plants 148
Along the Shore 149
Marshy and Wet Ground 149
Swampy Areas 149
Shallow Water 150
Water Plants 151
Underwater Plants 151

Animal Life in and on the Water 152

Below: A jewel among the gardens of Tuscany: Gamberaia in Settignano, near Florence. Jeanne Ghyka, Princess of Serbia, bought the villa a century ago and changed the vegetable garden at ground level into the mirrored water gardens that can still be admired today.

Right: A fountain pool, rising above the larger pond as shown here in the blue Majorelle Garden in Marrakech, is the focal point of almost every garden in the Arabic world.

Fascination with Water

The History of Ponds and Brooks

Anyone who tries to reconstruct a garden from memory will find to his amazement that he particularly remembers the water in the garden—whether it is the richness of water lilies, the splashing of a brook, or the peace of a fish pond that impressed him.

Water does every garden good. It fills the pond, brook, or pool; it makes the plants grow and bloom. Water leaves no one unmoved. It can be powerful or it can have a tranquilizing effect. It conjures up flashes of refreshing charm, reflects the passing clouds, mirrors the romantic moon. Water can be merry one moment and unfathomable or even worrying the next moment. But it is never boring. Stepping into the garden, every observer is drawn immediately to a splashing fountain, a brook, a pool, or a pond, as if led by an invisible hand. Only when one has seen his fill of the water does one take an interest in other details of the garden—the handsome pergola, the fragrant roses, the herb garden, the pleasant terrace.

The enthusiasm for water in the garden is widespread and has a long tradition. In highly cultivated lands, gardens with bodies of water were cultivated in ancient times. Among the oldest are the gold- and silver-ornamented water channels of the Incas in old Peru, some 2500 years before Christ, or the Egyptian palace gardens with their water basins full of lotus flowers. In the Far East, water has had a widespread symbolic meaning. The Chinese see the water surfaces in their gardens as reflections of the heavens, as a "way of heaven to come down to mankind and become visible." In Japan, it is said that water brings peace and quiet to the soul of man.

Water's diversity is found in other ways as well: lively, refreshing bright colors and powerful sounds, for example. In the splashing fountains of the gardens at Sans Souci in Potsdam, Herrenhausen in Hannover, or Versailles near Paris, water is

Modern modesty: This rectangular garden pool—two feet deep, with a border of pressure-treated wood—dominates an enclosed garden in De Rhulenhof, Holland. Two round bushes before the gate in the hedge and two tall trees by the house form an impressive frame (Ierssel).

flung into the air and draws all eyes to its constantly fascinating performance. In places where water has been naturally in short supply, such as Arabia, India, or Spain, it is used in more poetic and sensitive ways. One example worth visiting is the Moorish gardens of Alhambra in Andalusian Granada. Here, water becomes music as it flows out of softly murmuring springs into slim marble troughs and passes through the rooms and courtyards.

Natural Layouts
Versus Formal Gardens

For many centuries, the geometrically formed garden was regarded as the ideal. Indispensable components were tree-lined boulevards, flowerbeds, springs, pools, and fountains, all laid out symmetrically. At the beginning of the eighteenth century, interest in these gardens decreased. The taste of the times converted to the style of the landscape garden.

This revolutionary innovation began in England. Around 1730, the architect and gardener William Kent (1685-1738) was "the first who jumped over the hedge and saw that all of nature is a single garden." Many romantic gardens, marked by the spirit of the English landscape garden, came into being then. One of the most famous and most beautiful is Stourhead, in the English county of Wiltshire, where a river was dammed to make several lakes. The idea of a landscape recreated by people soon attracted great interest in the European continent as well. A notable example from those times is Munich's English Garden, which was created two hundred years ago by Friedrich Ludwig von Sckell (1750-1823) in the Isar Meadows, "for the purpose of movement, social recreation and approach by all classes." The focal points in the formation of such layouts were watercourses, dammed to make serpentine lakes, as well as trees that were planted in large groups. The idea was to imitate nature as genuinely as possible.

Ultimately, this type of landscape garden also made its way into private ownership. People no longer wanted to do without the charm of a tasteful, natural-looking waterway in a garden. The French impressionist Claude Monet (1840-1926) made no exceptions there. Monet, who had won fame for his paintings of water lilies and romantic river landscapes, noted, "One is not permeated by a landscape within one day. . . . And suddenly the magical aspect of my pond made itself known to me. I reached for my palette. And since then I have not changed my model." The painter proved his point impressively with many pictures, created on the basis of his self-planted garden at his home in Giverny.

Water as a Part of Modern Garden Architecture

In the present-day garden, too, water is of much significance. The size of the plot plays a secondary role—more important is the "genius loci," the spirit of the place. This includes the location of the plot, its landscape connections, the climate, and the native flora (including the existing trees). Also important are the architecture of the house, the materials it is made from, and the overall impression it provides. One must decide whether the garden is to be a true-to-nature landscape or have an architectural impact. These decisions will help determine the type, size, and location of the bodies of water.

Just as varied as the plots and their owners are the owners' expectations. When it comes to garden ponds, one person will prefer crystal-clear water, another wants a fish pond, still another chooses a natural pond. Should it be a swimming place in which one can go bathing? Or just a little pool because there isn't enough space for a "real" pond? For every ecological garden pond (without too great a fish population) there is the issue of equalizing the vigorous return of natural wetland development. Just think of all the village ponds that once existed. Such imitation biospheres do not succeed indefinitely in making up for the changes to wetlands and bodies of water. But they do offer urgently needed habitats for many species.

For many garden owners, a pond is most beautiful when it inspires luxuriant vegetation, as in the spring when the marsh marigolds display their glowing yellow blossoms. With a pond, completely different kinds of flowers are brought into the garden, and this very enrichment repays the effort that building a pond requires. The vegetation that flourishes in damp meadows, in swamps, or in (and under) water is simply fascinating. Although flowers are

especially colorful from March to July, a pond remains alive in the truest sense in autumn and winter. From a flat shore or a bridge, life and growth in a pond can be observed pleasantly, illustrating the very unity of nature. Forms of life that thrive at the pond go out into the neighborhood in search of nourishment. Frogs, turtles, and salamanders, to say nothing of dragonflies, do their part in the natural war against insect pests. And when a loam-containing area on the shore is kept open, swallows help themselves to the loam that they need for building their nests. Even when the pond is but a small one, its existence helps to stabilize the ecological balance.

A modern pool in beautiful old garden art: several varieties of roses are planted in pots set among the many trees (Beyers).

Claude Monet had a Japanese bridge with a graceful superstructure built over his pond in Giverny. With its overhanging growth of flowering grapevines, it became one of his most frequent motifs and gained worldwide fame.

Above: Art deco in Portuguese garden art. In 1935, the Frenchman Jacques Greber created a garden with impressive taste and striking architecture at the Casa de Serralves in Oporto. Now open to the public, this garden uses water as a central theme.

Below: In good British tradition, the dark green hedge forms an outdoor room, in the center of which—laid out symmetrically with the green walls—rests a peaceful round garden pool.

Ponds Must Be Beautiful
But Also Practical

The modern extension of a garden pond is generally regarded as a "swimming pond," which refers to swimming in a natural pool. It is considered the combination of a swimming pool and biosphere, thus becomes a swimming pond. To be sure, one can swim in any pond with a suitable depth of at least four feet, but in the new swimming ponds the area in which one can swim and the area which includes the planted border are completely separated from each other underwater. Visually, a large surface of water remains, with reeds and other swamp plants emerging from its sides. The comfort of such an open-air pool is considerably greater than that of an actual pond, because the water is clearer and one is not swimming among plants. The planted shallow-water area also serves as a source of energy, as the water warms up to pleasant temperatures in summer.

An enrichment of a very different kind is provided by a brook. It splashes and gurgles and brings movement into the garden, and with its homogeneous course through the grounds it provides a pleasing link between spring and pond. Small cascades, dams, embankments, and waterfalls create enchanting interest as well as a restful sound of flowing water. Not to be overlooked is the harmonizing of weather differences created by bodies of water existing in a radius of three to three hundred feet. The water makes the air cooler and more humid and reduces any excessive temperature variations in the air. In addition, those who look at a brook or garden pond from a financial point of view will be amazed to see how economical such a body of water is. The costs of the layout as well as the later maintenance are remarkably low.

More demanding—because they have to be cast in concrete or built of expensive materials—are the new garden pools or basins, the classic water formations. Whether designed with round or angular forms, as lengthy water channels or symmetrical reflecting pools, all complete the architecturally designed garden ideally. The possibilities seem to be unlimited, for in garden culture as in other designs, a mixture of styles is quite all right as long as it is done purposefully and not half-heartedly.

Planning and Building with a Garden Architect

Garden owners are often at a loss to find the right solution that is appropriate to their house and land. Hobby gardeners and homeowners who are inexperienced in garden planning should not incur risks when it comes to planning their garden. They will often save themselves time and money if, at the right time, they seek the advice of a specialist: a garden and landscape architect.

Such professionals can be used for all-inclusive planning, which includes all steps from sketchy first impression to finalized plan, planting, overseeing of all the work, cost controls, etc. Partial jobs, like draw-ing up a design, are also possible. The sooner a garden and landscape architect is included, the more effective his involve-ment will be.

Balanced and well-proportioned, the body of water is a focal point of this garden in Provence. Before the lengthy swimming pool, flanked by two elephant sculptures, lies a flat "bed of water" that can be planted.

A pond need not be large to have an emotional effect, but it can be, even in the garden of a row house. And a brook can glide by silently or dominate the garden area. Large or small, near the house or far from it—in all cases, pond and brook can combine effectively with the garden architecture, and, ideally, with the architecture of the house as well. The twenty-five garden scenes that follow illustrate how that look can be achieved in all its versatility.

The Loveliest Ponds and Brooks

The plan: the waters reach right around the terrace by the house. Beginning at the spring, the brooklet flows into the broad pond, in which one can swim. Scale: 1:400.

Upper right: A nice view from the garden: the house and the large pressure-treated pinewood terrace in front of it seem to float above the water.

Center right: The narrow brook opens up beyond the wooden bridge into a fairly large pond, its shores gently giving way to a lawn.

Lower right: Everything in yellow: the monkeyflowers (*Mimulus*) along with lady's mantle (*Alchemilla*).

Design: Garden Architect Kurt Lehrke, Koenigswinter

If the homeowner alone had decided, the yard would have been transformed into one big waterscape. But the landscape architect called on for guidance advised against a large lake. His position: The proportions of house and garden would no longer balance. In his design, the architect guaranteed plenty of play space in the liquid element and planned the water surfaces so that one had a view of the water from all rooms looking out on the garden. Sometimes the water is just a narrow brook that splashes over stones, in other places it spreads out to several feet wide. Here it is about four feet deep, thus offering the opportunity for swimming. To ensure that swimming will be fun, as well as for other aesthetic reasons, it is desirable to have the water as clear as possible. This was achieved by using a four inch thick layer of turf, which was stamped onto the bed of the pond and covered first with a layer of sand, then of gravel. It also helped to lead all rainwater through the small spring into the pond. The species of fish chosen to live in the pond helps reduce the numbers of gnat larvae.

Waterproofing: EPDM pond foil

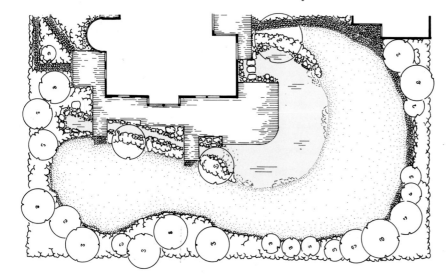

Around the House: Almost Nothing But Water

Below: The water offers an inspiring play of light and shadow, thanks to the lofty treetops. Swamp plants, such as marsh marigolds (front) and water plantain (*Alisma*), grow well in semi-shade and make the edge of the pond disappear.

Right: This house from the fifties, its many-sided facade reflected in the pond, was extended by a modern building complex in truly striking architecture (Architects: Spengler, Wiescholek).

Design: Landscape Architect Beate Hojda, Hamburg

The location of this pond was developed from several different perspectives, as the reflections in the water were meant to be visible directly from the living rooms and workrooms. Since the angle of view is greatly extended by the large, high terrace areas, the pond had to be pushed as far as possible into the garden and the planting on the banks reduced. The root areas of the lovely old trees (birch, beech, oak) helped to determine the shape of the pond; its extension was laid out gently among the tree-topped areas. Thus the greatest possible effect of depth was achieved.

For reasons of safety, the pond bottom includes a berm, measuring approximately one-half to eight inches thick, all around; it is formed as a planting zone for swamp plants. In order to achieve a balanced water temperature, the depth of the water was limited to approximately seven inches. The substrata for the plant zones consists of half topsoil and half sandy material taken from the pond and is ten to fifteen centimeters thick. To keep the pond clean, about a hundred fresh-water shellfish, which obviously reproduce, were introduced (although no fish were used). To date, the water shows no murkiness.

Maintenance: Dead plant parts are removed; the many leaves are removed in the autumn with a fishnet that is attached to the nearby trees. Tent pegs anchor the net to the edge of the pond at intervals of three to six feet.

Waterproofing: PVC soft (Plastoplan), 1 mm thick
Substrata: garden soil thinned with sand (taken from the pond)

Romance under the Trees

The plan: the large water surface was not linked to the terrace, so the sunny area could become a lawn and the view from the house to the water would not be obstructed. Very carefully, the pond pushes its way among the old trees. The clay figure (left) is by Leni Nordmeyer. Scale: 1:400

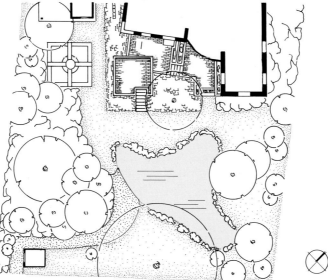

Below: One looks across boxwood and moss to the house with its terrace and artistic pond, whose liquid mirror is filled with blossoms and trees. On the island (behind the stone lantern), dwarf Weymouth pines that were shaped twenty years ago grow among the flowering cherries.

Right: Opposites are the basis of the planned scene here: tender blossoms next to the Japanese maple, long-needled pines beside garden bamboo. The pond forms a restful spot in the center of the garden.

Design: Studio Renate Richi, Braunschweig

In the beginning there was a gravel pit. It lay eighteen to twenty-four feet deep between the newly erected house and the romantic woodland scene—a relic of the gravel business. What was to be done? The whole landscape could not be shaken up, or the supporting wall would have grown too high to see over. The thing to do, then, was to create different levels and garden areas, and, despite the porous underground, plant them with shrubs and plants like azaleas, lavender heather, or rhododendron. As a painter, the garden planner saw the lot like a canvas on which a colorful, lively picture was to take shape, one in the manner of a Japanese garden—a type of garden that Renate Richi finds particularly charming.

The house itself is considered a part of the whole, an area from which one can experience the garden and feel close to nature—viewing the water, the playful goldfish, the sparkling frogs and dragonflies sunning themselves on the water lilies, and the waterfall. A winding path with a projecting terrace provides the transition to the garden. From here, one comes down several wooden steps onto the most important level of the garden, where the pond, up to three feet deep, was created. In the pond are a romantic island and a Japanese-style stone lantern. The banks are planted with azaleas, pines, and shrubs. In April and May, when the blossoming cherries, azalea, and rhododendron are mirrored in the water, the garden is indescribably beautiful. For the owner of this garden, it can never be more beautiful during blossom time than at home.

Waterproofing: Reinforced concrete

Change: The Garden Becomes a Picture

Below: The fine and tender blossoms of the azaleas and the rhododendron hybrids offer a lively contrast to the bright green of the ferns and maples and the powerful tones of the pines.

Right: In a colorful blooming garden, green tones are important; here they come primarily from Weymouth pines, Norway spruces (*Picea abies*), and bamboo.

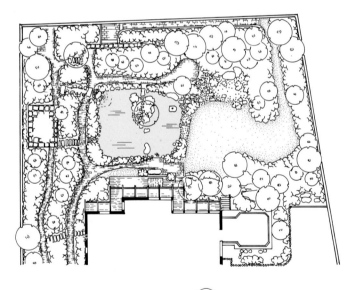

The plan: from the slightly raised position of the house with the pergola-terrace before it, one looks upon the pond with its peninsula. At right, the lawn leads into the lower area, which was designed as a rhododendron valley. Scale: 1:600

The plan: The striking design of the long pond makes the green area look even better. The brook's course, up to six feet wide, stretches over ninety feet of the land. Scale: 1:300.

Right: The lawn rising up on both sides gives the brook a beneficial width. Since the water scarcely flows along, a dreamy water reflection is created—almost like a pond.

Design: Helga and Johannes Roth

At first fleeting glance, the deception is perfect. Is this long body of water a brook, or more of a pond? Following a longer look, the answer is still not definitive. In fact, a brook is created in the wide sweep of lawn, acting even more like one when the circulation pump is turned on. The reason for this deceptive play: because of the meager slope, one scarcely notices that the water flows. The body of water, some ninety feet long, has been formed in the manner of a Japanese dry landscape. During the first few years, it was really just a dry brook bed. But since the water formed puddles here and there after long periods of rain, the owners decided in favor of a striking new treatment. They started over again, almost from the beginning, and rebuilt their stream bed. What would have been senseless on the banks of many ponds became a formative refinement here, carried out with good taste. In lieu of thick planting, the banks of the pond were lined with large and small natural stones, forming a striking transition from water to green grass. Since the owners of the garden planned the layout themselves, its realization took a great deal of time; an entire summer vacation was taken up just building the border of the brook.

The unusual shape of the pond works well with the planting: a carefully chosen mixture of bamboo, pines, dawn redwood (*Metasequoia*), and dogwood (*Cornus*).

Waterproofing: Foil
Depth: 15-20 inches; width: 0.5-6 feet

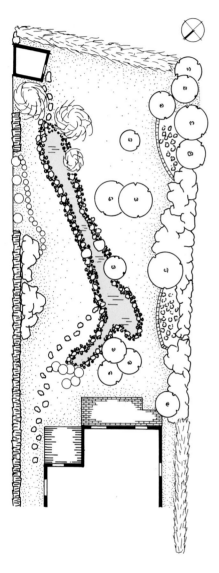

A Brook Like a Pond

A bird's-eye view shows the artistic course of this waterway in the style of Japanese garden formation.

Right: An uncommon type of brook: it winds it way through almost the whole garden and is bordered by very few scarcely blooming plants. The border is instead comprised of boulders and smaller stones.

Below: The paved path (of basalt) leads directly along the pond. The sandstone blocks cleverly conceal the concrete wall that secures the edge of the pond.

The plan: a romantic path leads through the nearly natural planting of the house and the large pond. A way station is formed by the square sitting area, which is often the end point of a walk around and offers the nicest view over the water. Scale: 1:300.

Right: The large sitting area, twelve feet square and built on beams, projects out over the water and invites one to stay awhile. An old apple tree provides the necessary privacy.

Design: Grün plan, Rüdiger Weddige, Volker Lang, Hannover

When a garden is to be redesigned, one has two choices. The least expensive choice is to proceed carefully and just correct the existing layout here and there.

More expensive, but more effective and more convincing in the end, is to develop a concept with new ideas and plans. Here the builders let their landscape architects convince them and decided in favor of the second way. The results shows a sensitively conceived pond that defines the nearly natural garden. At six feet, the pond even has enough depth for swimming. Ecological means have been used to make the pond bottom watertight: clay tiles, built to

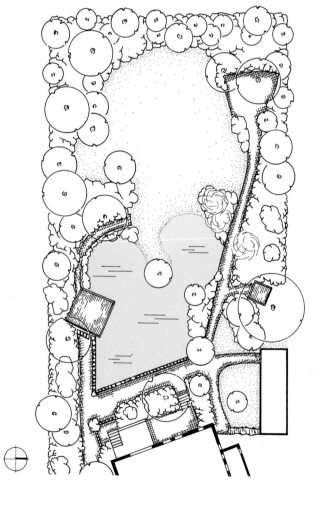

The Pond as "Garden Center"

overlap in two or three layers, were stamped firmly in place. The shore nearest the house has been structurally defined by a concrete wall covered with sandstone blocks (used material). The shore areas lead to the garden more naturally. The square sitting area made of pressure-treated wood projects over the pond like a footbridge and is very inviting on summer evenings.

Waterproofing: Clay tiles (Dia pond-building elements) on geofleece

Below: Every single stone was carefully chosen and laboriously set in place—which was not so simple, for the positions could be chosen only during construction.

Right: In the space created by carefully shaped pines, azaleas, and rhododendrons (which cleverly conceal the nearby construction), the rock formation was made into a waterfall. Here the brook follows its course and fills the two ponds.

Design: Garden Architects Ulrich and Hannelore Timm, Hamburg, with Günter Kynast.

"A garden must grow to become that which makes it valuable," is an aptly stated phrase. And this includes the growing of the shrubs, flowers, and trees. But here, something else was just as important: the garden had to start growing before it existed—during its planning. Only then could it develop into a size that would last a long time.

The whole thing began with the garden architects' concepts. This plan envisioned a stretched-out pond beneath the big, layered terrace, over which a bridge (or a wooden footbridge) was to lead into the garden and to a place to sit. The garden owner went into detail, thought about the plantings. After the plan was carried out, the family was happy with the harmonious shape of the pond. But after a few years, the owner, Günter Kynast, missed an optical counterweight to the pond. Ideas were discussed with the garden architects and a new set of plans were formulated. This led to a flowing brook and a waterfall, which now make the garden look charming, even in the less noticed parts. Heavy boulders, individually chosen in a quarry, were used to build a rock formation six feet high. From its highest point, a brook's course begins, and from there down, the water makes its way into the pond. It flows over additional boulders and through slim channels into the pond. The daily joy provided by the garden justifies the long hours of planning and the amount of work.

Waterproofing: Polyester and pond foil

Ripe Time
For a Garden

The lightness of a Japanese garden finds a European variation here. Gravel and flat stones are carefully arranged, grass grows softly to the water's edge, and the reflections are lavish.

A plan that was created in two stages: first came the terrace with the steps, the pond, and the path to the sitting place. Later came the waterfall with the brook, which makes this part of the grounds so exciting. Scale: 1:300

A view across the steps, the boulders, and the round boxwood goes deep into the garden and lets one forget that this plot is not very big.

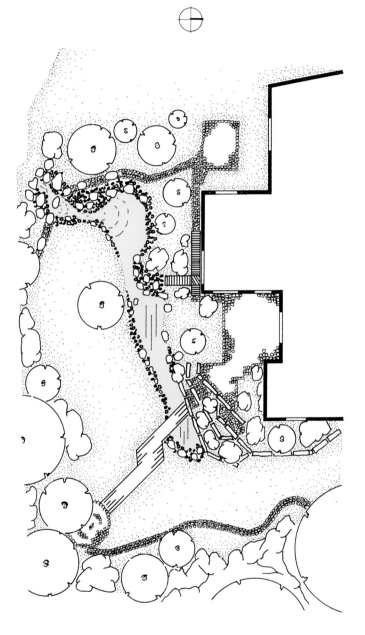

A harmonious transition from the terrace by the house across the steps and brook to the garden, in which the pond and the brook became the central theme. The waterfall can be seen in the background.

Below: In the first year of renovating the garden, the plants along the shore are dominated by the remarkably luxuriant pontederia. The bridge in the middle, three feet wide, opens the garden to the visitor.

Right: In the second year, the green of the swamp plants and the first flowers of the buttercups and flowering rushes are already flourishing. The flat pond offers an inspiring view and interesting flora.

Design: Henk Weijers Gardens, Haarlem, The Netherlands

A garden can frustrate you. The view from the living room is disappointing when you have to look at high water basins instead of flowers and greenery. What was planned at first as an enrichment of the home's terrace, and then made real, soon turned out disturbing. In addition, the area to the rear offered nothing that made a stroll through the garden worthwhile. A new concept was needed fast, and one in which the water would take on a major role. In place of the too-high water basin, a flat pond was designed to border on the terrace. The homeowners could do nicely without a lawn. Thus arose a large water landscape, twenty-four to thirty inches deep and planted in one part, and five feet deep (deep enough for swimming) in another part. In order to observe the garden—or more precisely the pond surface—from nearby, wooden footbridges were added. Everything has straight lines and is very practical, qualities that Hollanders are accustomed to from their land reclamation. A footbridge, forty-five feet long, was built along the living room; another bridge of more than sixty feet leads to the back part of the garden. The plants were chosen to be appropriate: nothing fanciful, nor any mixture of various shrubs just to have something blooming all year long. The prescription: a unified choice of plants lets the garden create a grand effect, and increases— after a sometimes long interruption—the joy of blossom time.

Waterproofing: Pond foil with attachments of bongossi wood

Wide Ponds Instead of Pools

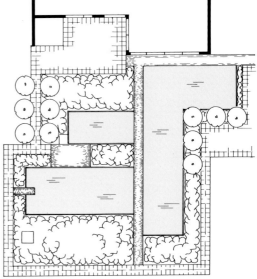

The plan: square corners and straight lines define the manner in which the terraces, paths, and ponds are laid out. The strict arrangement is slightly eased by the swamp plants. Scale: 1:400

The plan: from the small pool, water winds its way among boulders and gravel to the big pond below. From the sitting places in the lower garden, one has a splendid view of the water and the reflected "blossoming" path of steps. Scale: 1:500

Right: This example shows that doing without big lawns allows one to experience more of nature in the garden. Various spots offer inspiring views of the water and the house. At right, salvia invites the bees to nectar.

Design: Garden Architect Christian H. G. Wegener, Hamburg.

The situation is typical: when a garden gets old, thorough renewal becomes necessary. How long this development lasts is determined by the planning and by the chosen materials and plants. The reason is understandable, as often just a small budget remains for the garden after the house is built. As a result, low-priced flat rocks are bought and fast-growing plants are planted, and after a short time one is dissatisfied.

When the garden architect was given the job of reorganizing this garden, only the small pool and the already-existing trees were to be retained. The changes in the garden area were made carefully, and when completed, they harmonized quite naturally with the shrubbery before the terrace. From the overflow out of the small pool near the terrace, the brook accompanies the path of steps into the garden, crosses it, flows over boulders, and then pours into the pond. From there, the water is pumped upward again. It was important to plant flowers that would bloom at almost any time of year, or at least bring out something charming. A mixture of shrubs and a few trees was chosen, fulfilling all wishes for flowers from spring to late autumn.

Waterproofing: Pond foil, with sand under the stones in two layers (for detail, see page 147)
Material for paths and steps: granite pavement and secondhand curbstones

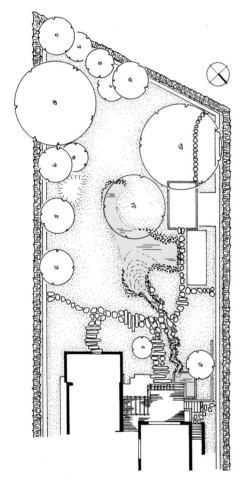

After Ten Years: A Facelift for the Garden

Left: The view from the house to the garden is attractive not just when the azaleas and lilacs are blooming. The changing picture of flowers, grass, stones, and reflections in the water provide a new effect every day. The carefully designed mouth of the brook and the shape of the pond also contribute to the overall effect.

Right: Autumn atmosphere by the pond: while the shrubs and many plants seem to outdo each other in color, the needles of the yews and pines retain their constant green.

Lower right: Natural stones and the brook's course harmonize well with the screen of bamboo, the decorative maples, the flat-growing bugle (*Ajuga*), the saxifrage (*Saxifraga umbrosa*), and the Japanese azaleas.

Below: This section of the slightly lowered channel shows how a few well-arranged stones soften its hard lines in a charming way.

Design of terrace and channel: Architect Wolf-Eckart Lüps, Utting. Design of pond and plants: Landscape Architect Wolfgang H. Niemeyer, Munich.

That a house forms a unity with its garden is not yet taken for granted. The uncertainty about which components of the architecture can or should be carried over to the land is too great. The undertaking requires a thorough understanding of materials and colors, structures, and the whole wealth of available vegetation. When the result is to be unified, architects and planners must cooperate and be ready to compromise. In this garden, the house architect and the landscape architect actually shared the work. The architect planned the terrace, with its curves that gently release it from the house. A deep row of plates at the end of the sitting area serves as a water channel through which the water, with a minimum of grade, slowly flows into the pond. The landscape architect took responsibility for the pond area and its plants. He chose a harmonious combination of fruit trees and shrubs, such as red maple, magnolia, pines, willows, and rambling roses. He also used shrubs that lengthened the blossoming time: purple loosestrife, larkspur, and poppies.

Water in Dialogue with Architecture

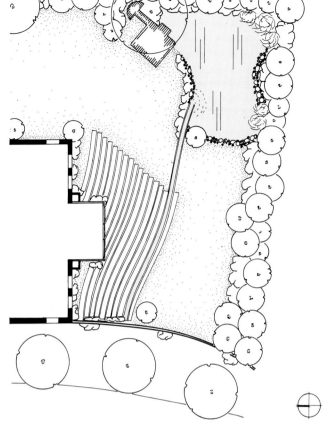

The plan: in an unusual way—not straight, not round—the terrace opens into the garden and toward the pond. Scale: 1:250.

Spring in the still-young garden by the house: narcissus blooms in the meadow, accompanying the water that flows calmly from the terrace down the gently curved channel into the pond. What still seems transparent will develop in the coming months and bring the garden to its own vibrant life.

41

The small pool, some twenty inches high, mirrors the already present form of the octagonal terrace. One looks across the spillway to the yellow flowers, the water, and the patch of open woods.

Right: Out of the pool, which was made of granite blocks, the excess water is directed to the brook over a polished granite spillway.

Design: Garden Architect Christian H. G. Wegener, Hamburg

This lot in the area of a terminal moraine shows its singular character: although the land is basically wooded, great parts of the house and yard lie in bright sunshine. Thus, a good view of the crowns of the pines, birches, and oaks is afforded without having to stay in their shadow; on the contrary, on hot summer days it can be too warm on the terrace and in the conservatory. On such days, one gladly seeks a place to sit in the light shade.

The garden architect's plans included a brook bubbling around this terrace, flowing in a constant curve. Two other terraces below the house enhance the first, and create the possibility of seeing the water and the house from different points of view. These three sitting places are linked with each other by flat or split boulders. As steppingstones, these boulders lead through the flowerbeds, along the brook, or across the water. Thus one comes also to the newly planted areas in the light shade of the trees, a combination of azaleas, ilex, ferns, wood grass, and wild shrubs.

An electric circulation pump set in a special water reservoir provides the necessary movement in the brook and pond. For ecological reasons, all the water from the roof is channeled into the brook.

Brook and pond waterproofing: Pond foil and sand layer

Water Brings Movement to the Garden

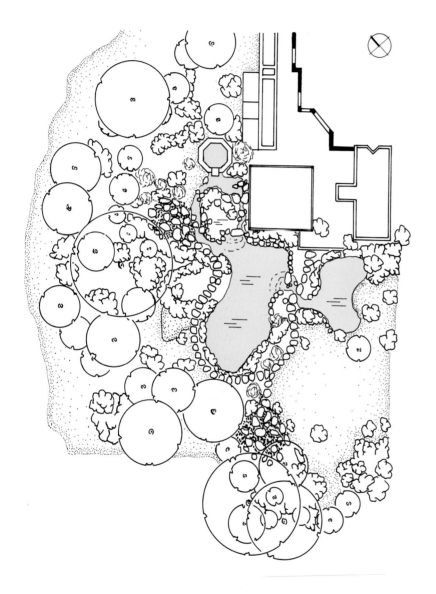

The plan: sometimes narrow, sometimes wide, the water surfaces reach out onto the yard. One can reach the various parts of the garden via steppingstones, viewing the house and pond from new angles along the way. Scale: 1:300

Right: Around the conservatory and the roofed terrace behind it, the brook and pond spread out on the wooded grounds. The small octagonal pool can be seen between the glass structure and the maple tree.

Below: In front of the house is a lot of pond, planted with pontederia and water plantain. In the foreground grow the yellow-blooming ligularia.

Upper right: In the jungle of swamp and shore plants, bamboo, and ligularia, is a raised seat of wood, to which one can withdraw and feel hidden.

Lower right: From the house, one looks out at the rectangular pond and the patio, which was hidden away behind the painted wooden wall. The tiled roof in the background is that of the garage and carport.

Design: Henk Weijers Gardens, Haarlem, The Netherlands

Some properties provide a challenge for the builder, and particularly for the garden planner. (for the homeowner, it is then simple to pass his requirements on to the garden architect he hires.)

The problem with this lot was simply its location: the part of the garden worth mentioning stretches between a heavily traveled, inner-city main highway and the house. It is, to be sure, the sunny side, but it is unfortunately quite affected by the noise from the traffic. In back of the house are the entry and a fifteen foot wide strip fronting on a narrow neighboring building.

What could be done about all this noise? Wooden walls almost six feet high were erected, and a high earthen wall was created and heavily planted, reducing the noise to a general rushing sound. Behind these walls, a garden could now arise in which one could enjoy spending time. The garden architect planned it as if it were newly-gained land—all in straight lines without a curve. A rectangular pond (twenty-four by twelve feet) is the nucleus of the garden. A wooden footbridge, three feet wide, leads from the house between the side terrace and the pond into the garden. An angular path of flat stones takes over here and leads around the bamboo and grass thickets back to the house. The unusual feature of this garden: despite its straight lines, it does not seem at all severe, but rather original and, thanks to its unified, scarcely varied planting, very harmonious.

Waterproofing: Pond foil, fastened with bongossi stakes

A Garden Straight Off the Drawing Board

The plan: here everything is reduced. The planning for the garden is dominated by a strict grid, composed of a wooden footbridge and concrete plates, which cut almost through the center of the garden. Very few materials and types of plants were needed. Scale: 1:250

Just one year after its planting, the garden is taking on contours. Now the high white sight and noise barriers are still visible, as are the sitting areas of red concrete slabs and the footbridge that almost cuts the garden in half. In a short time, however, the plants in the pond and beds will spread out and mask the severe sectioning. A nice romantic effect will then characterize the garden and its pond.

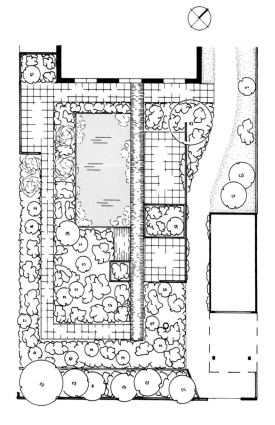

Below: The walkways of wooden planks and natural stones invite anyone who would like to cross the pond to relax and admire the surroundings.

Right: Trees and flowers bloom between the natural stone by the house and the pond, joined by small works of art. These include the sculpture *Swinging Stone* by Nobuko Sekine, which rests on a stainless steel column in the water.

Design: Garden Architect Dr. Ivan Ruperti, Aldesago, Switzerland.

When an art collector seeks out a plot of ground for himself, he thinks clearly of what sculpture, what object should stand where. When that person is also a garden architect, he has still other reasons to choose a very special plot of ground. For all such reasons, the owner of this land—who practices both professions—decided on a former vineyard in the Italian part of Switzerland.

The slope first had to be evened out and a three-foot wall braced, before the ground could be made usable enough to create the large pond desired by the owner. Thus arose the possibility of placing the actual garden on one level. It now spreads out below the house (Architect Ivano Gianola) and before the conservatory. It is delightful to descend a few steps and then walk along the shore promenade. The pond, up to thirty inches deep, offers a varied area along its shore, where large and small stones alternate with plants such as iris, bulrushes, and peonies. Even turtles feel at home here, and spend the winter under the layer of ice that gets as thick as fifteen inches.

The paths in this garden could not form straight lines, but had to run in zigzags. The reason: based on the mythological Japanese garden, evil spirits get left behind on such paths. The spirits can only go straight ahead and are thus kept away from the house and its occupants.

Waterproofing: Pond foil

Lots of Pond and Slope

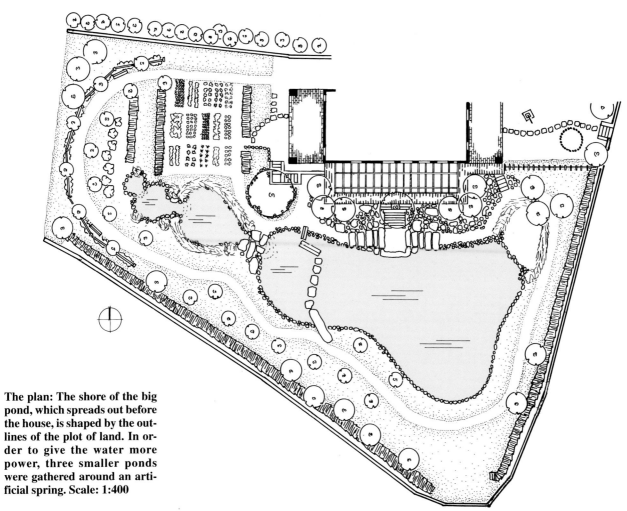

The plan: The shore of the big pond, which spreads out before the house, is shaped by the outlines of the plot of land. In order to give the water more power, three smaller ponds were gathered around an artificial spring. Scale: 1:400

Below: Iris, one of the loveliest flowers for pond shores, bloom around May, usually at the same time as rhododendron. Along with the swamp spurge, they grow near the wooden planks and give the foreground a glowing color.

Right: With many dam levels, the speed of the water is checked. Surrounded by flowerbeds, the slow moving water forms beautiful reflections.

Design: Boedeker, Boyer, Wagenfeld & Partner, Düsseldorf

They have become rare, those really big lots in the midst of cities. But now and then they do turn up, like this one, which was once an orchard. The grandfather had bought some five acres of land, planted and maintained it—now his grandchildren and their children can enjoy the space. The small house grew into a villa and the orchard became a cultivated garden.

All this took some time. The garden developed over a period of more than ten years, bringing the individual areas "into shape." At first, the formation of the entry area, the terraces, and sitting places by the house were important. The water was considered as well: a lengthy pool was placed on the sunny side of the house and a large pond with natural atmosphere was placed at the lowest point of the landscape.

Only many years later did the natural connection between the two bodies of water come about: a brook's course. It now winds its way gently through the sloping land, accompanied here and there by luxuriant vegetation, until finally flowing into the pond. In order for the plants to develop, they first had to be protected by wire for an entire summer to prevent wild animals from eating them!

Brook and pond waterproofing: Pond foil

The Brook Makes the Yard Even Lovelier

Four years after planting, the flowers along the brook have developed into a magical wealth of blossoms. Lady's mantle (*Alchemilla*) and day lilies (*Hemerocallis*) combine with dwarf bamboo to form a splendid frame for the artificial course of the brook. The red steel sculpture was created by Wolfgang Goeddatz of Cologne.

The plan: Nothing more remains of the onetime orchard. Many trees and shrubs give the garden a fine park atmosphere, and the brook—beginning up at the terrace—cuts through the broad lawn. Scale: 1:600.

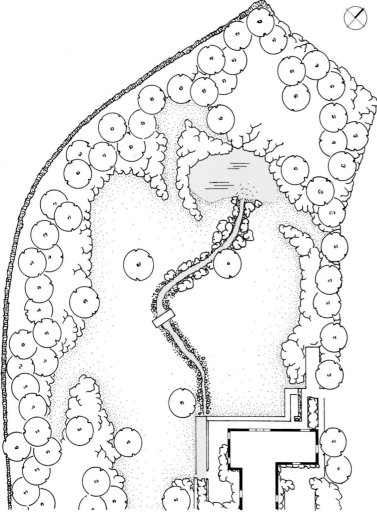

The plan: On the spreading lawn, several areas were formed in the style of Japanese garden art. The broad pond with its waterfall is often the destination of a stroll through the garden.

Right: Water, stones, and plants create an artistic atmosphere in the light shadow of the lovely trees. Areas of tranquillity are thus formed amid the big garden—places for meditation, consideration, and dreaming.

Design: Reiner Jochems (Roji, Japanese Gardens), Bernd Breitenbach, Berlin.

It is said that a big garden is easier to plan and lay out than a small one. Accordingly, this area of more than two acres should not have been much challenge for the builders. But the reality was quite different.

The owners of this large piece of ground, which contained a splendid growth of trees, wanted a garden with Japanese atmosphere and much water. They found two garden planners who had experience conceiving Far Eastern gardens and who understood their ideas. To be sure, the planners had never worked on a piece of land this large. They made plans, threw them out, and made new plans, until the three essential ingredients of a Japanese garden—water, stones, and plants—existed in the right relationship to each other. Additionally, the two garden planners took on the job of actually carrying out their plans. It took weeks to move all the soil—somehow, almost four thousand square feet of pond surface had to be excavated! Planting was held back. The garden required several focal-point areas, but allows many views from the house.

The water lies far from the house, which appears especially charming. It became customary for the builders to visit the property every day and examine the land during every rainstorm. Water occurs here in many ways, as a waterfall, a flowing brook, and a pond. In the tea garden, formal pools were created in genuine Japanese style. When visitors wash their hands here, it is said that the class differences of the participants are put aside during the tea ceremony.

Waterproofing: Clay tiles

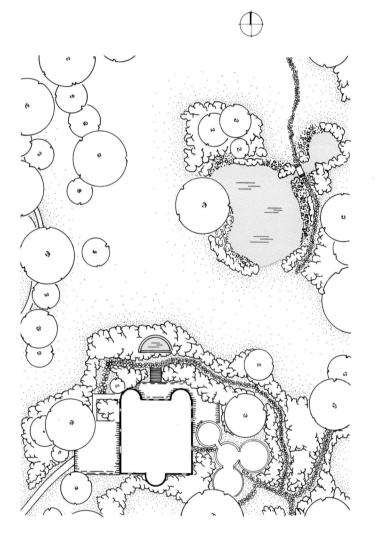

Japanese Garden Culture for a Pond

Right: The location of every boulder, every steppingstone, and the accompanying stone bridge has been carefully planned, resulting in a most harmonious impression.

Above: From the cascade behind the pond, one enjoys a view over the stretch of water, extending back to the Zen garden with the tea pavilion and the house right next to it.

The plan: The rounded ponds are bedded in the park landscape. They lie some distance from the house, but are very inviting. Scale: 1:900.

The house and garden form a wonderful unity, especially on hot summer days when the clouds are reflected in the water as if on a postcard.

Pages 62-63: Instead of colorful flowers, green tones alternate here. In the background is a poplar boulevard, in the water are bulrushes (*Scirpus*) and water lilies, in the foreground are the huge leaves of the gunnera (*Gunnera*).

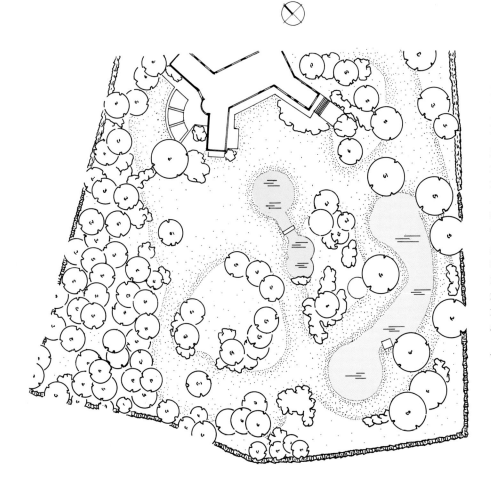

Design: Architectural Bureau Landscape & Garden, Solingen

One of the nice features of being your own boss is that you don't have to work on a schedule. What is much more important for the garden planner is that, besides a certain amount of understanding of nature and form, he or she needs flexibility and ideas. On the one hand there are the builders' wishes to fulfill, on the other hand, the job of bringing them into harmony with the nature of the land.

In the renewing of this great garden (bearing the dimensions of a park), distance had to be created first. Too many trees and shrubs had been planted, now needing to be pruned or felled. In addition, an adjoining, newly bought cornfield had to be integrated so that a unified garden could result. A pond almost two hundred feet long was planned, reaching far into the greenery in the form of an angled coat of arms. The pond bottom was dug out to a depth of up to nine feet. With such depth, the water can regenerate itself better in the long run and it is more advantageous for the fish. Separated from the first by an earthen hill lies another pond, the middle of which can be crossed via a bridge. A laborious but worthwhile measure was further included: the grass in front of the house was removed to a depth of approximately two feet, resulting in a nicer view of the pond. Concurrently, this provides a good vantage point for viewing the impressive house and its appropriate surroundings.

Waterproofing: Pond foil on fleece

Ponds in the Cornfield

Below: Between the house of steel and glass and the forty-five foot rock wall, the six foot deep pond forms an oasis. From the balcony, one can observe the animal kingdom: during the day, many ducks pay a visit. One summer, three young foxes were born. Bats live in the grottoes and lizards climb on the rocks.

Right: The architect could not have handled the demands of a piece of land better. The transparent building is open to light and affords a dramatic view of the rugged rock wall with the pond deep below.

Design: Bambek & Bambek, Stuttgart

"A clever attempt to bring about the meeting of nature and modern technology in an unusual place. Before a rock face in a vineyard and a small pond stands a house that, thanks to its building materials—mainly metal and glass—sets itself off decisively from the structures around it." This excerpt from the jury's verdict for the coveted Hugo Häring Prize in 1991, given by the Bund Deutscher Architekten, describes the project featured here splendidly.

Previously, the condition of the land was sad. It gave the appearance of an untended backyard in a quarry that had closed down in 1938. Even before the garden was planned, the rock face was cleaned of loose rock, one part over the grotto was anchored, and the whole thing was strengthened with sprayed concrete.

To create the pond, the ground was dug out to a depth of approximately six feet and waterproofed with foil. Three bags of mud from another lake made it easier for the water to become a wet biosphere. Marsh

The Pond by the Rock Face

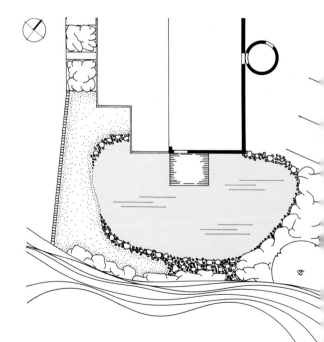

The plan: The pond, over thirteen hundred square feet in area, fills the space behind the house. Although little light comes in, plants and animals thrive. Scale: 1:300

marigolds, reeds, various water lilies, duck-weed, and waterweed were planted. Two waterfalls (helped by circulation pumps) provide the necessary oxygen for the carp, goldfish, turtles, lizards, and frogs that live in the pond. For both animals and plants,

the yard has been made into an oasis in an otherwise overcultivated and polluted environment.

Waterproofing: Pond foil

Below: An idyllic transition from the pressure-treated, pine terrace to the path covered with wood chips: roses, larkspurs, and mallows provide colorful blossoms by the pond.

The plan: The terrace and the pond compete for dominance in the garden. There is much wood by the house, allowing one to choose a place to sit that takes best advantage of the sun's location. On a path, one can stroll around the lot and observe the pond from all sides. Scale: 1:250.

Design: Landscape Architects Volker and Helgard Püschel, Mettmann.

Sometimes there are patches of green that make it imperative to link nearby surroundings with the garden design, as their appearance or that of their trees so enriches it. The majority of the lots currently built on, however, must get along without these no-cost gains. The builders have to make the best of the lot itself. In this case, the owners needed their garden architect to dampen the noise from a nearby playground for children as well as to prevent people from looking in. When the desired pond was planned, privacy was very much taken into consideration. Concrete walls three feet high separate the planted earthen hill from the neighboring properties, their ground levels having been raised when the pond (approximately three feet deep) was first dug out.

A World in Itself: Pond Landscape

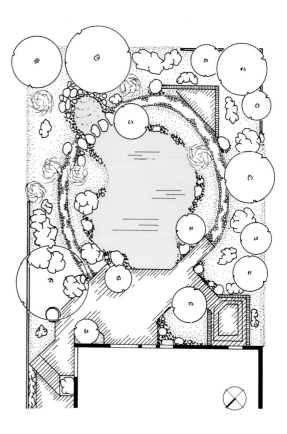

The builders wanted to forego a lawn and a play area, as the owners' children are already grown.

The terrace by the house is the central place to spend summer in the garden. From there, a path covered in wood chips takes one to another small sitting place and to the mini-waterfall, which is supplied with water by a circulation pump.

Waterproofing: Pond foil

Almost the whole garden can be seen from this view. In summer, just a few months after the spring planting, the pond, the plants, and the two wooden terraces offer a nearly complete picture. The spring at the left rear and the two spring stones let one hear a pleasant splashing and also supply the water with oxygen.

Below: A living hilly landscape, up to four feet high, its effect enhanced by romantic ponds and fountains, lets one forget the nearby buildings and street traffic.

Right: Over steppingstones and carefully designed footbridges made of American red cedar, one is led elegantly over the water to the sitting area in front of the pine trees. Those with time to spare will enjoy a new impression of a Japanese-type garden here.

Design and construction: Inspired by Nature, Munich.

Nowadays, there are more and more lots that look very nice but are situated most unfavorably. The reasons for this are many; in this case, the proximity of a superhighway caused the problem. First of all, the loud noise is a nuisance. Though one may get used to it, it still has a negative effect on the resident's well-being. Secondly, the fast auto traffic in the area creates a "contagious" sense of frenzy. The garden, therefore, should be designed to provide a quiet contrast.

What was to be done? The planners turned to a natural style of formation, like that common to Japanese gardens, with water as the dominant element. Indeed, water plays a decisive role here. In the form of a pond with depths up to five feet, it is transparent and playful; as fountains and waterfall it is strong and energetic, pleasantly covering up the traffic noise. Just the proximity of the garden to the superhighway is enough for visitors to find it restorative—nature is close enough to touch. In addition, the water raises the humidity of the air, thus improving the climatic conditions. The planting is also based on Japanese models. New impressions keep emerging, thanks to plant groups and hills. Sometimes the observer gains a deep insight into the scene; sometimes the hills and rocks (the latter a blend of greenish quartzite and yellowish-white crystalline marble) conceal the depth of the garden. Thanks to intensive planting of the shallow-water zone (which represents about a third of the water surface) and the use of unfertilized turf balls, the water is nearly algae-free after three years.

Waterproofing: EPDM pond foil, 1.5 mm

Impressive and Very Japanese

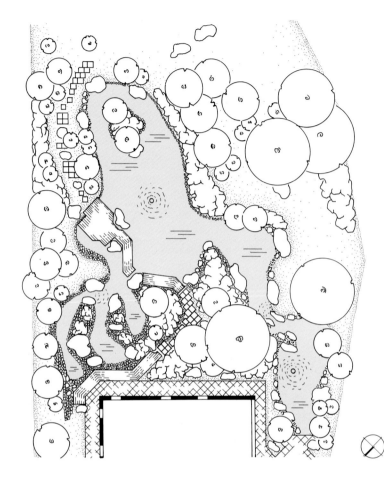

The plan: water flows through the entire lot. It is laid out in refined Japanese style, sometimes narrow and unpretentious, sometimes wide and imposing. Scale: 1:400

Below: With the exception of the reflected fountain, everything here is round: the unworked boulders, the lawns, the paved shores of the pond. Everything blends together, becoming a truly complete unity. The high point is formed by the vigorous fountain.

Right: An island of peace? The windblown spray from the fountain in the background creates an obvious but pleasant sound. Visitors are happy to be immersed outdoors, able to behold plants like these rhododendron from close up.

Below: This pocket-size garden has become an attractive scene. The pond fills nearly all the garden's width and ends just before the sitting area.

Right: The large pond and the thick planting of pine, bamboo, and reeds make one forget how small this lot really is; the reflections on the water convey the impression of far more spaciousness. But that is not a disadvantage!

Design: Landscape Architects Rheims & Partner, Krefeld

Regarding the question of to what extent ponds enliven a yard, row house gardens typically give poor answers. As a rule, owners will opt for a body of water that is essentially little bigger than a basin. In this yard, however, it turned out quite differently. When the garden architect offered the builders his design, which converted practically the whole yard to a water landscape, the whole family responded—after only slight hesitation—with a big "yes." This, they felt, was just the way their boring garden should be restructured. From the enlarged terrace by the house, a path now leads via steppingstones across the pond to the sitting area opposite. From there, the family can look back at their own house—not just at the neighbors. Carrying out the plan turned out to be quite complicated, as there was no place in the narrow yard for the soil that was dug out to make the pond; it had to be taken away completely. Even the bamboo plants could not stay where they were growing; instead, they had to be separated and transplanted.

The idea of sharing the garden with the family's neighbors on the right was considered, but this project must wait until their children are old enough to safely enjoy the water.

Waterproofing: Pond foil

For a Row House: Water is Prettier than Grass

The plan: The narrowness of a row house lot, this one barely eighteen feet wide, still offers enough space to build a large pond that can be "crossed" on steppingstones to a pretty sitting area. Scale: 1:200

The plan: The expanse of this garden plot results from alternating heavily planted areas with open lawn and water surfaces, allowing a long view. Scale: 1:500

Upper right: A nice view of the water, which extends between the blooming catalpa tree (*Catalpa bignonioides*) and bamboo to the lawn in the background.

Lower right: The mood of a Japanese garden is amplified by the sitting area, which was built on a wooden deck in front of the garden house. The thick planting on the opposite shore brings added privacy.

Design; Landscape Architects Wolfgang R. Mueller & Partner, Willich

This garden was laid out in three stages. The basic concept was created first, consisting of a spring and small pool near the house. Then came the garden house—a separate building for celebration—complete with the water garden shown here. The grounds were modeled with distinct differences in elevation, designed to give the pond area a natural frame. In addition, the thickly planted earthen hills provided essential sight and sound boundaries. The owner had come to know and love Far Eastern gardens on his business trips to Japan, and wanted to adopt several of their features, such as the choice of plants and the varied ways of utilizing water and stones. Between the trees, a large pond filled with water lilies, steppingstones, and Koi carp was created. The picture was completed with a spring, a waterfall, and a Japanese fountain, the water flowing into a small brook. Putting up a summerhouse added another touch to the creation of a Far Eastern landscape.

The last phase to date includes the creation of a tennis court and a prairie garden. With every change of the garden, the owner's knowledge of plants and natural connections has increased. Often, not only does the development of a garden take time, so does that of its owners.

Waterproofing: Asphalt mastic underneath a three-inch layer of tarred gravel (due to the inclusion of heavy stone blocks)

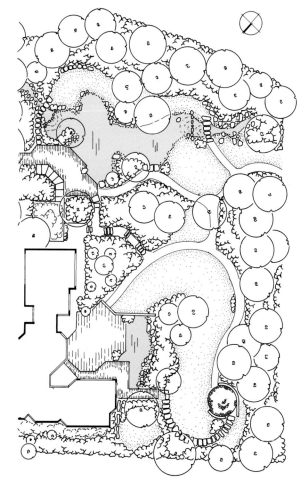

Water Landscape, Natural Experience

Below: A view across the water shows a bridge with white railings, leading to the patio in front of the rebuilt teahouse. Lady's mantle (*Alchemilla mollis*) and Pacific Island silvergrass (*Miscanthus floridulus*) can grow almost without limit.

The plan: Clear lines determine the concept of the garden on this land. A patio by the house, a central path to the teahouse, a pond and a path around it. Scale: 1:400.

Right: From the sitting area by the pond, one enjoys a view of the rural garden and the house. The pond and the old fruit trees blend harmoniously, and the temporary fence in the background (put up to protect the children who cannot swim yet) is scarcely disturbing.

Design: Garden Architect Siegmund Behr, Celle

Circumstances like these are not hard to find: a house and garden getting on in years, both bought by new owners. Regarding the half-timbered house, the current owner had no doubt as to what was needed: it was renovated and returned to its original condition as much as possible. The garden, however, was a different story. Overgrown, it contained only a few old fruit trees and a little summerhouse that had once been a chicken coop.

The new concept called for different use as a family and relaxation garden. By the house, a large terrace was planned, including space where the children could play.

Renewing a Garden Grown Wild

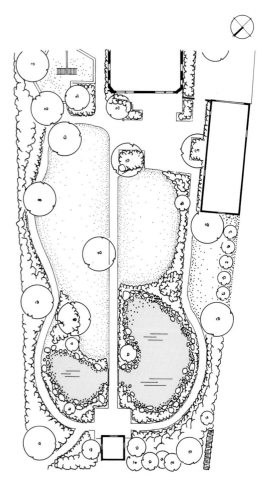

In the back part of the garden, a large pond with a bridge was added. The latter leads directly to the ex-chicken coop, which was to be rebuilt as a teahouse with a place to sit in front. The owners took to this idea with enthusiasm and had it implemented at once. Surrounded by luxuriant greenery and the pond (up to three feet deep), a relaxing garden corner was thus created, complete with a fine view of the house and garden. The wooden bridge and brick paths link this spot with the other parts of the garden. A necessary precaution: as long as the youngest child cannot swim, the pond is fenced off. But it will not be much longer until the fence can be removed and the garden attains its final appearance.

Waterproofing: Pond foil on a four-inch layer of sand
Pond enclosure with lawn-bordering stones set in concrete, over which foil was laid.

In this plan, the dimensions and formative ideas were clear: The terrace in front of the house was symmetrically and clearly laid out; the strict form relaxes by the pond, a component of the romantic nature garden. Scale: 1:900

Lower right: The terraces are a stately white, with the pond spread out before them. To keep the harmony from becoming *too* perfect, a few angles are broken by steps and walls.

Right: The symmetry and balance of the house are reflected in the large terrace. On the other hand, the adjoining pond has been given a natural border shaping.

Design: Landscape Architect Peter Neuberger, Fürstenfeldbruck

The turn-of-the-century villa had changed hands and been renovated; the garden was next. For a long time, the property, more than two acres in size, had been used as a deer park. The condition of the trees was predictably bad.

In planning the new garden—unfortunately, neither old plans nor formative elements of the land existed—the landscape architect decided in favor of a classic style with symmetrical path connections. The large terrace of crystalline marble slabs was planned in two levels and based on the symmetrical axis of the house. Before the lower

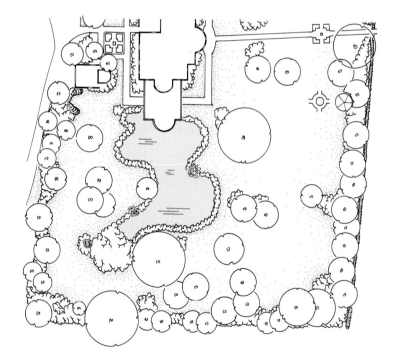

Classic Modern

level lies a large pond. The angle of the view is a basic formative element here, linking the strict, ordered part of the garden by the house with a considerably larger part of the property, which has been kept natural. This natural garden not only offers an exciting contrast, it also meets the ecological requirement of providing living space for animals and plants. The principle of opposites has been used in other places, finding expression in the adaptation of historical formative elements: angles in the terrace, walls, and steps and the relaxing of symmetry in several other areas lead to the opposition of classic forms with free forms. This kind of garden architecture—the questioning of retained forms—can be understood as a part of the spirit of our times.

Waterproofing: PVC foil, 1 mm; terrace: crystalline marble, 50/50; enclosing walls and columns: concrete Dyckerhoff white sanded

The plan: In reworking the property for use as a garden, nicely rounded, natural shapes were chosen for the terrace by the house, the patio, and the new pond. Scale: 1:500

Right: How naturally the pond curves between the fruit trees and gives way directly to the large lawn. In the background the house may be seen, with the sitting area at the right.

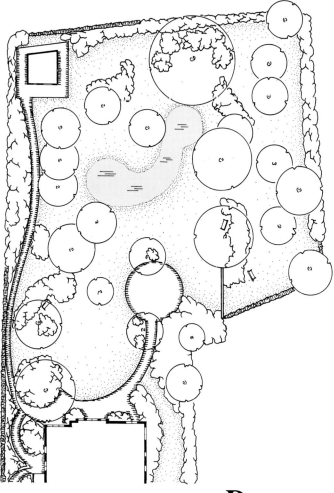

Dreams under Trees

Design: Architecture Bureau for Landscape and Garden, Solingen

The former fruit orchard was originally a spruce forest, but that was a long time ago. After a change of ownership, apple, pear, chestnut, and plum trees, as well as birches, oaks, and ashes were planted. This, too, was thirty years ago. Then the property changed hands again, and the land was to open into a landscape for use as a garden. Many old fruit trees had to be felled and others replaced by younger ones.

What was lacking in the level garden was a body of water, which was to take on the spreading landscape typical of the lower Rhine. It was not easy to find the right place in the yard for a large pond without having to sacrifice a tree for it. The result was a long curving form that kept proper distance from a pear tree and ended in a circle with a diameter of more than fifteen feet. Even though the water surface is rather small in comparison with the entire property, a very different impression is formed when one walks through the garden—here there seems to be plenty of water. Is this a result of the dynamic shape of the pond? Whatever the reason, the deception has succeeded.

Waterproofing: Pond foil, laid on a protective fleece

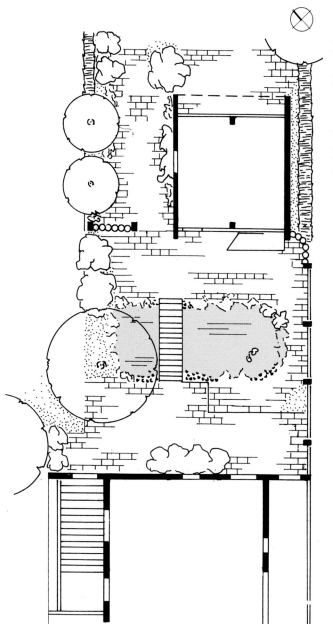

The plan shows only part of the long property, in which an area between the house and garage has been made into an inside courtyard with a pond. Scale: 1:200

Right: The rectangular pond lets the area between the two buildings become an attractive garden courtyard. The step interrupts the flat surface and enlivens its structure while the footbridge links the two shores.

Lower right: Between the warm and sunny brick areas, the goldfish-inhabited pond seems mysterious and cool. The shore plants and shrubs form a friendly transition.

Design: Architect Klaus Rudloff, Norderstedt

This lot has its problems. The biggest: it is some two hundred feet long. How does one use such length? By building one structure behind another. And that's what the owners of this narrow lot have done. Between the street and the garage in the rear, a wide driveway and parking area for additional cars was built. Almost forty-five feet behind the garage is the house, with the terrace on its southwest side. For years, though, the open space between the garage and the house was nothing but a monotonous passage from one to the other. The brilliant idea was to put a pond with a wooden footbridge in the middle.

The large area was paved with a type of bricks that come in varying sizes, giving a rustic effect. The pond measures about thirty by twelve feet. Although most ponds of this size are only thirty to forty inches deep, this one is unusually deep—up to three feet. The footbridge, made of pressure-treated pine, is attached to two beams that rest on masonry abutments. This will last and withstand the weather. The pond foil was attached on the sides so that there is a small border for water's edge and swamp plants. The dividing line was made almost neutral with gravel.

Waterproofing: Pond foil

Without a Snorkel

The plan: like rays of a star, the footbridges depart from the home's extensive terraces, leading across the pond's landscape to the path around the yard. Scale: 1:400

Right: From the house, one has a lovely view across the ice to the snowy woods and garden pavilion, which encloses the sauna.

Design: Team Grün-Plan, Wehrheim

Two lots, used only on weekends for thirty years, were completely renovated and revamped. The existing building could not be torn down, but was rebuilt instead into a studio, with a new house being built in wood-pillar style. The grove of birches and firs was thinned. To even out the great height differences of the land and create a usable garden and pond area, up to four tons of heavy diabase rock from a nearby quarry were brought in and placed along two rows. On the pond side, two thirds of the rocky ridge is underground, and the rocks serve as "steppingstones." The ponds, conceived as a "walkable" water landscape, are linked by wooden footbridges and steppingstones—and especially enjoyed by children. The water surfaces consist of two ponds at different levels. The upper one receives the runoff from the roofs and drainage systems. The excess water then flows into the lower pond, which is located by the sauna and serves as a swimming and diving pool. It also provides water for the garden and toilets.

In the small square pool by the brick terrace, there is a copper kettle under the water (see page 87). The circulating pump that is installed in it makes the water overflow on both sides. Thus, a contrasting play of water art exists along with the nearly natural ponds, in which even an island with its own biosphere has been built. And of what garden can it be said that in winter it is almost at its loveliest?

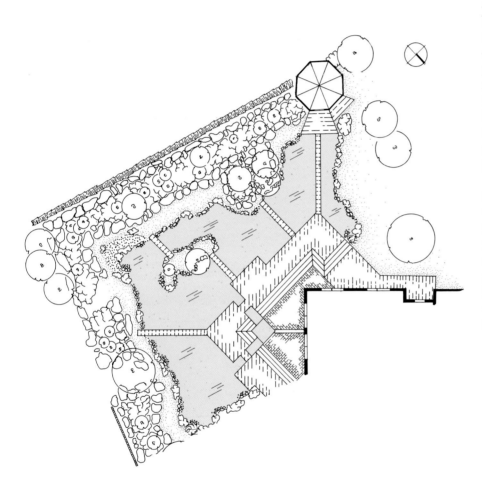

More than a Winter Fairy Tale

Waterproofing: 1-mm pond foil was laid on a two-inch layer of clay and sand and a protective fleece. In the lower pond, this is topped with a four-inch layer of clay and sand, and at its edges a twelve-inch layer of material from the pond bottom, without loam or humus. On this is a four-inch layer of approximately three-inch diameter diabase fragments. In the upper pond, water is led via drainpipes into a concrete pipe of more than three feet diameter, filled with .5-mm lava pieces. It is clarified by a special planting.

The thin covering of snow turns the pond landscape into a romantic winter fairy tale, one in which the pond surface plays an important role.

The numerous narrow footbridges connect house and garden very cleverly, not disturbing the expansiveness of the water landscape at all. On the contrary, in fact, they lure the owners and their guests outside, inviting them to cross to the far shore and experience the gardens in all their variety and naturalness.

Between the brick terrace and the steps of western red cedar is the small square pool, from which the water flows through copper ducts in two directions. From the lower terrace, a multistemmed ginseng tree rises.

This picture illustrates how the precisely drawn shapes, the brick terrace with its mosaic inlays of Carrara marble, the wooden terrace, and the footbridges, alternate with almost pure nature—the water landscape with its many stones, plants, and fish.

Lots of sky and an inviting swimming pool are offered by this big pond. The planted area on the shore is optically linked with the swimming area, which extends from the wooden footbridge. The whole scene has the atmosphere of a small lake (see next page).

Swimming in your own pond is really the most natural thing in the world, as long as the pond is big enough and deep enough. But only a few garden owners have the "courage" to do this; for many, unchlorinated pond water is too dirty or too cold or otherwise unpleasant. People swim in swimming pools built for that purpose, though some are often all but indistinguishable from a "normal" pond—thus they can be included easily in a garden layout. The water can be kept clear by the plants in it, and it is much warmer than one thinks. The following pages illustrate the variety of possibilities for swimming in your own pond.

Ponds for Swimming

Below: Everything is very natural: the dry wall that keeps the wind out and the sun's warmth in, the flat stones of the patio, the wooden pier, and the "swimming pool." The water temperature rises in summer to 82° Fahrenheit.

The plan: The large "swimming pool" is laid out so that it receives lots of sunshine and can be seen easily from both the house and the garden. The portion used for swimming is about one third the entire water area. Scale: 1:700

Right: The pond merges harmoniously with the fruit orchard. In the foreground, the separation between the swimming area and plant area is easy to see. The swimming pier was made of untreated larch, which rests on pillars.

Design and Construction: Biptop Landschaftsgestaltung, Weidling, Austria

Charming Burgenland, southeast of Vienna, offers spacious properties with nearly natural greenery. Often one can scarcely tell the private estates from the public green areas. Anything that might significantly decrease the natural quality has been avoided. What was to be done, therefore, when the owners of such a property wanted a place to swim? The entire water area of some two thousand square feet was located at the lower end of the property, at the bottom of a slight slope. This was the most natural place to build, for water always gathers at the lowest point. The soil that had to be excavated for the pond was used just beyond it for additional support. The swimming area, about five hundred square feet, was made six feet deep. Below water, it is separated from the shallow, planted border area by an earthen wall. In the so-called regeneration zone, where the swamp plants grow, the water is cleaned biologically. In addition, it gets warm here much more quickly than in the deeper area. In all, twenty-five kinds of swamp and water plants were planted in this wide shoreline zone.

Waterproofing: Reinforced pond foil, 1.2 mm, laid on a protective fleece

A Swimming Paradise Behind the House

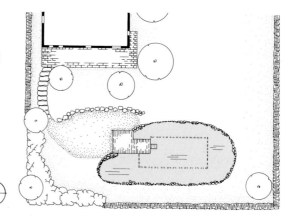

Below: The view from the house—along the small rose garden—shows the new swimming pool down the slope. The planting, still sparse, needs more time to develop.

Right: Visitors see almost nothing but blue sky as they swim in the pool, which measures thirty-three by twenty-four feet. In the foreground is the underground platform at the pool's entrance; behind the boulders is the handsome skyline of the city of Graz.

Design and construction: Angelika Kern, Albin Gilma, Graz, Austria

There are properties which clearly make the question of where a swimming pool should be placed a challenging one to answer. This plot, with its fairly steep downward slope, old fruit trees, and glorious view of the city, is just such a case. At first, the idea was to build a small swimming pool directly in front of the house. After long discussions, the family decided to take advantage of the property's size and build a scenic swimming pool on the slope. The swimming oasis was to be located about two hundred feet from the house. Connecting the living area with the swimming pool turned out to be problematic, however. A wide pathway winding downhill was ultimately laid out, one that a riding lawnmower could traverse. At the pond, the owner specifically wanted a straight-line step. The shape of the pond was excavated from the slope, and the bottom filled in with building stones. Since the surface was large enough, a natural-looking pond with an area of five hundred square yards could be constructed. The six-foot-deep swimming area within the pond measures thirty-three by twenty-four feet. It is separated by an underwater earthen wall from a shallow area, up to nine feet wide, that contains swamp and water plants. At the pool's entrance, four steps lead to a small platform under the surface. Swimming here is especially pleasant and comfortable.

Waterproofing: 1.5 mm PVC pond foil on a base of sand and geofleece
Wooden terrace: 1.5 inch pressure-treated boards

Open-air Pool with a Long View

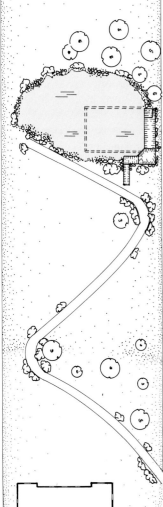

The plan: Thanks to its great distance from the house, this pondscape of more than five hundred square yards has the effect of an independent recreation area. The athletic-minded owner goes swimming here until October. Scale: 1:700

93

The plan: this large lot, which continues into the next without a fence, was enhanced with a large swimming pond. Scale: 1:600

Lower right: The sitting area made of larch invites one to relax "in the harmony hidden in living stillness," as the designer likes to say. The inclusion of the rocks in this area adds charm—and saves wood.

Right: Heavy fieldstones were integrated into the pond shore as things to look at or look from, adding to the overall effect.

Design and construction: Inspired by Nature, Munich

Many properties—certainly including this one—can scarcely be made more beautiful than in their existing, natural state. Gently rolling meadows out of which mountains rise here and there, combined with a wonderful view of the lofty surroundings, are worth more than the best planning. To be sure, such a lot would be even more perfect if it included a small lake for swimming—one that would look attractive as well. So, what was missing was added—the swimming pool. The spot chosen was just a little distance from the house, reachable by a few natural steps. In order to leave nature as untouched as possible, big fieldstones were integrated into the wooden patio area and some were put into the water as well. The pond was given a sufficient depth and an entrance for swimming. In summer, when the sun shines long enough, the fresh spring water is warmed, inviting one for a refreshing swim. The result is what designers hope to achieve for each of their gardens: an open space created for the human spirit, in which the senses, exhausted by everyday life, can gratefully recover.

Waterproofing: Pond foil

Swimming in a Mountain Meadow

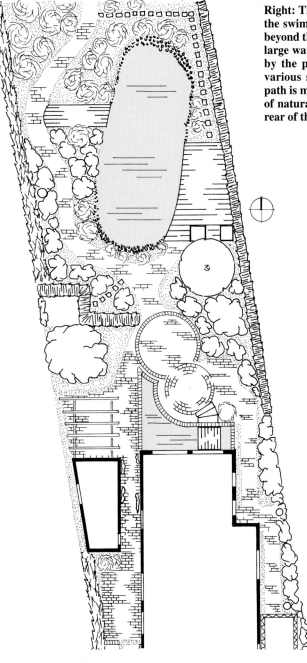

The plan: the swimming pool, measuring some fourteen by thirty feet, fits nicely into the garden. The terraces and sitting areas break up the large areas of planting. Scale: 1:200

Right: This bird's-eye view shows the swimming area, which begins beyond the hedge at left front. The large water surface is surrounded by the planted areas, with their various shrubs and grasses. The path is made of a colorful mixture of natural stones and leads to the rear of the garden area.

Design: Michael Müller, Bramsche

With all due respect to an inheritance, not everything can be kept exactly as it is received. But what is worth keeping and what can be discarded? Those who take over property from their parents are always faced with this decision, and the owner of this long garden plot was no exception. After the old house had been remodeled, renovated, and refurnished, the owner saw nothing but boring grass in the garden. The solution: a swimming pool. Making this happen turned out to be more complex than anticipated, for the soil had to be dug out by hand to a depth of about four feet. The work was made easier by the fact that the owner was himself a partner in a professional landscaping and garden-building firm. On the right side of the garden, just behind the plum tree, enough space for the terrace with a bathhouse and shower was soon found. The filtering system is built into the little house nearby. As in a "genuine" swimming pool, the water is sucked by a skimmer and sent through the filtering system. From there the water is piped through solar panels on the garage until it splashes over a few stones and back into the pool. Swimming is fun here all summer long—and in winter, the pond is a fine place to skate.

Waterproofing: Pond foil, attached to bongossi wood strips four inches wide all around the edge. The openings in the pond foil made by the screws allow excess water to overflow.

Swimming Pool:
A New Look
for the Garden

Early summer: past the small pool by the house and the rhododendrons into the swimming area. A catalpa tree in front of the hedge in the background catches the eye.

From the evening sitting area one has the nicest view of the swimming terrace with the two bathhouses and the shower between them. One serves as a changing cabin, while the other conceals the filtering system that enriches the water with oxygen.

Still life by the beautiful, but still rare black bamboo (*Phyllostachys nigra*). Here the filtered water flows back into the swimming pond.

Below: The restrained planting by the house allows a nice view of the pond: large yellow loosestrife (*Lysimachia punctata*) grows under the tree, and in front of the conservatory is lady's mantle (*Alchemilla mollis*).

The plan: the new garden concept focuses completely on the four thousand square foot swimming pond. The remaining ground is laid out simply as lawn. Scale: 1:550

Right: The pond shore meets the lawn gently, as in this spot where an old tree trunk lies rotting. A raft—the garden's special attraction—is anchored in front of the wooden platform. In the background are the rolling hills of grass.

Design and construction: Angelika Kern, Albin Gilma, Graz, Austria

The planning sequence that led to this pond was not unusual: a house in an older development was modernized and, thanks to a built-on conservatory, made more attractive. Then the garden needed to take on a new face. The idea of integrating a swimming pool into it was inspired by the existence of an excavation on the property and the urgent wish of the family's three children to swim in their own yard. When the nearby brook overflowed its banks and flooded the low-lying part of the yard, there was plenty of water on the property anyway. . . .

The swimming pool was kept near the terrace so that the children can be watched conveniently when they swim. When the soil was dug out, the lower-lying land was raised and two nicely curved hills of lawn (seeded with playground lawn mix) were created; they are easily mowed with a power mower. The entire pond covers four thousand square feet; the swimming area measures thirty-three by twenty-four feet and

More Fun on a Raft

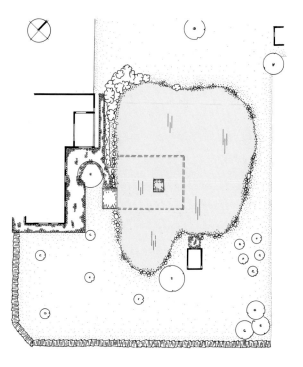

is separated from the shallow swamp and regeneration area by an earthen wall. So that adults can swim here in comfort here as well, the depth of this area reaches almost seven feet. A small path leads from the terrace by the house and the conservatory to the wooden platform with its entry ladder.

Here a raft, six feet by four feet, was built for the enjoyment of the children and their many friends. It is secured to a concrete anchor in the pond.

Waterproofing: 1.0 mm PVC pond foil on geofleece and sand layer

The plan: the large pond area, which has become the center of this natural-like formation, distinguishes the back garden area. Scale: 1:400

Upper right: The concrete wall separating the thirty-six by fifteen foot swimming area from the planted section can be seen clearly here. Thirty different species of swamp plants decoratively cross the dividing line. In the foreground, the planting gives way to the flower meadow, while in the background are the wooden footbridge and the sunning area.

Lower right: The footbridge over the two-hundred square yard pond is an invitation for sunbathing. The plants around the pond were limited to the shore areas, where the water warms up to pleasant temperatures.

Design and construction: Biotop Landschaftsgestaltung, Weiding, Austria

This attractive spot had one big disadvantage: looking out from the nice, remodeled house into the garden, one's gaze fell on the not very attractive, albeit utilitarian architecture of a railroad station. During the garden's remodeling, therefore, the burning question was how the new garden's aspect could turn one's eyes away from that view. The idea: design a "nature preservation area" with a big swimming pond in it. Thus a lively contrast arises, with the more elegant garden style right by the house. It was important to the owners to keep a group of spruce trees roughly in the middle of the property. They limit the panoramic view from the terrace of the whole garden—an advantage, because the yard then remains all the more interesting. The position of the "swimming pool" was determined by the sun and the character of the garden. The swimming pond was to be situated at the end of the yard, with everything laid out geometrically. This would create a refreshing counterpoint to the domestic planting. For guests, the pond is reachable by a footbridge, placed where the afternoon sun shines particularly long. The whole water surface measures two hundred square yards, of which an area thirty-six by fifteen feet is reserved for swimming. The pond opens toward the house and garden, and the greenery has been kept low in that direction. To the rear, towards the railroad station, everything is planted more naturally. Here a luxuriant flower meadow thrives, as do native shrubs and trees; in time, they will successfully block the view of the station.

Waterproofing: Pond foil, 1.2 mm, reinforced, laid on a protective fleece. The swimming area is separated by a reinforced concrete wall (underwater).

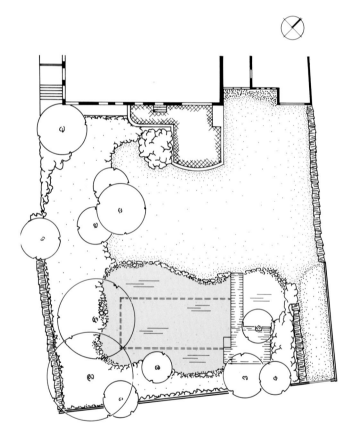

The Swimming Center near the Railroad Station

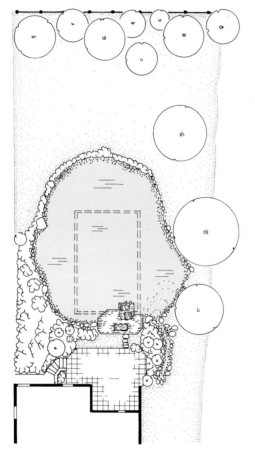

The plan: the large water surface of the swimming pond spreads out in the center of the front garden. The land opposite is farmland, allowing this unusual position right near the entrance to be used as a water garden. Scale: 1:300

Upper right: A charming entry: this wooden design with sun deck was necessary to bridge the distance of four feet between the terrace by the house and the water level.

Lower right: A good solution: despite the great height difference, one can go directly from the house into the water. The wooden terraces have been integrated into the slope with the large boulders. To the left, a small brook emerges from the fine gravel. Behind the cattails (*Typha*), the wall that separates the swimming area is visible under the water.

Design and construction: Angelika Kern, Albin Gilma, Graz, Austria

This swimming pond was developed in answer to the question: how does one make the best out of an unfavorably situated garden? The one-family house from the '50s is on a long narrow lot, almost ninety feet back from the street. Next to the driveway lay the usable garden area, with an elevation difference of some four feet to the terrace. The steep slope was overgrown with rock medlar and juniper. Right below is where the pond was to be built, with direct access to it from the terrace. The successful solution: the slope was modified with building stones (boulders) and the wooden terraces integrated between the stones. The upper, larger sun deck lies about one foot below the terrace. A narrow stairway then leads to the lower level. From this lower platform, one can jump into the water or climb easily down the entry ladder. Of the total water area (approximately thirteen hundred square feet), a portion twenty-four by fifteen feet was planned for swimming. The swimming area is five feet deep and separated from the rest by a wall that is ten inches thick and built on a concrete foundation. The wall ends about a foot below the surface. The adjoining planted regeneration areas, in which the water warms and restores itself, are between one and four feet deep and follow irregular contours. For both acoustic and optical liveliness, a brook has been added beside the terrace.

Waterproofing: 1.2 mm reinforced pond foil on polyfelt fleece and a sand layer

A Biosphere in the Garden

The plan: no lawn was planned at all here. Instead, the long, winding pond can be viewed from the house and makes the garden look bigger than it actually is. Scale: 1:500.

Upper right: Lots of water that invites one to swim. When the rhododendron is blooming, the pond is especially lovely. Goldfish have thrived here for years. They need no care and no feeding, but wipe out mosquito larvae.

Lower right: In and around the water, plants and animals live symbiotically, and the choice of plants was not limited to native species. From the narrow footbridge, everything can be seen in more detail.

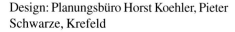

Design: Planungsbüro Horst Koehler, Pieter Schwarze, Krefeld

As different as houses and their facades are, so too are most of the gardens that go with them. The owners of this big property had a house built in the traditional style of the lower Rhine. Their garden was to be traditional as well, and include two focal points: first, a big, useful garden in which fruits and vegetables could be grown bio-dynamically; and second, a large pond in which one could also swim. In order to experience more of nature from plants, trees, and water, the owners opted to do without a lawn.

A place was soon found for the young vegetables, off to the side of the living space in the western part of the lot. And the pond? It winds through that part of the garden that opens in front of the U-shaped house. As in nature, the water sometimes comes close to the terrace, sometimes winds away from the house. A small peninsula is created, catching the eye and making the water area seem considerably larger. No particular entry is provided for swimming; one simply goes right from the wooden footbridge or the sitting area into the water, which is up to five feet deep. To add oxygen as well as pleasant sounds, the water is circulated via an electric pump and sent splashing back into the pond over a rock.

Waterproofing: 2 mm thick PE foil on a 4 inch layer of mortar

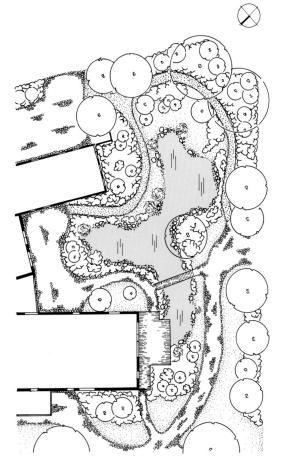

Swimming Amid Goldfish and Water Lilies

The plan: the outline of the house blends nicely into the big garden complex, in which water plays a dominant role; the proportions are visibly related to the architecture. Scale: 1:350

Right: Contrast heightens the charm of the garden, from the angled architecture and see-through wooden walls to the vibrant red maple and the natural granite block out of which the water springs.

Design: Jack Chandler & Associates, Yountville California, USA

From their efforts to integrate a building and its garden into a unity, many garden planners are familiar with this dichotomy: "On the one hand, it was necessary to take up the architecture of the house; on the other, I wanted to make my own presence clear." The California landscape architect assigned to this project was in a jam. His task included the reworking of the garden and—in particular—the already existing swimming pool. What could he do? The owners wanted a garden that required a minimum of upkeep: one that was practical but optically charming at the same time. Once Jack Chandler found the way, he delivered exactly what they wanted. The angular architecture of the house complex (Architect Mark Mack) is repeated in the entire garden design. Examples can be seen in the swimming pool, which was given a new rim and more sitting space; in the pergolas, which take up the materials and design of the balcony in two separate units; and in the low walls, which form the background for the water basin with its granite fountain. Or is the varied use of water the most vital element of the garden? Sometimes water fills the basin and lures one to go swimming; sometimes it is a refined little channel in the lawn (the decorative overflow of the basin); sometimes it is an especially decorative spring that bubbles out of a split granite block. One of the most essential design elements is the continuation of the color concept from the house into the garden, creating an impression of unusual harmony between house and garden.

Waterproofing of all water bodies: concrete

California Dream

The bodies of water at a glance (from left): swimming pool, water basin with granite block, and the scarcely visible channel in the lawn. The color concept for this California garden consists of few components. The focal points are formed by warm red tones, supported by strong green.

Below: The house and garden (if one can use that term for this area with the patio and swimming pool) form an architectural unity, both aesthetic and functional.

The plan: simple but persuasive, the spacious terrace stretches out below the steps. The thirty-six by seven foot swimming pool is integrated right into it. Scale: 1:350

Right: A dream view: the swimming pool, over seven feet wide and thirty-six feet long, was built cleverly into the slope, making the garden area look considerably bigger. The dark gray paint of the pool walls soaks up the sun's warmth and makes the water look deep.

Design: Architects Ross Anderson & Frederic Schwartz, New York

When an architect is to design a house for his parents, he is under especially great pressure to succeed; his clear concepts might easily overwhelm his parents. The task here was to create a house with a swimming pool on a sloping lot in the Napa Valley, California's renowned wine-growing area. The house should not appear too massive, and should fit nicely into the landscape, comprised of stables and sheds of the wine growers down in the valley. The result has a timeless beauty, for its grandeur is not ostentatious in the least. Rather the house, with its terrace, lets the architecture speak eloquently for both. So that the symmetry is not excessively perfect, it was "let go" a little outside. The sitting area on the terrace is a little to one side, and the pool was laid out right along the axis of view—thus attracting attention to itself. A fine job of letting this slim basin make the sloping lot useful.

Waterproofing: Reinforced concrete

Small House, Great View

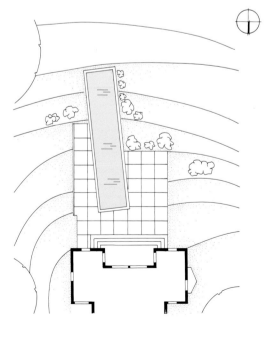

When one imagines a place where relaxing vacation days have been spent, or where it would be nice to spend some time happily sunning oneself, being refreshed, or just doing nothing—a swimming pool often comes to mind. With its elegance and lightness, a pool is the center of a seemingly carefree life, the very embodiment of a vacation ideal. The pleasure of a swimming pool, though, should not be limited to one's always too-short vacation time. As long as the property offers enough space and the climate is favorable, a swimming pool can enrich daily life and even serve as a meeting place for athletically-inclined guests.

Swimming Pools

Perfect garden architecture, American style: here a merry life can center around the swimming pool and everything that might please the eye has been thought of. The focal point is the glass bathhouse with the swimming pool before it. Just a few steps away to the left is the Jacuzzi whirlpool, while the raised area to the right can be reached via wide steps built into the lawn. (Jack Chandler & Associates)

When the climate allows year round swimming, a pool can be placed in the middle of a garden and thus be laid out centrally. Such is the case with this property in Florida, where the pool fits nicely into the U-shaped house design and can be seen from every room. The diagonal pattern of the red cedar patio planks is well chosen, as it gives this "open-air swimming room" more optical width.

Italian flair can also be found in the Rhineland, as in this case. Large, flat, natural stones, separated from each other by strips of grass, lead the way to the swimming pool. The thick hedge of laurel separates the swimming area from the rest of the lot. (Pietro Porcinai)

This swimming pool from the '60s was no longer being used. The water was clear, but the plastic rim looked unsightly. The solution: the entire area was surrounded with a railing (as on a ship) and thus turned into a pleasant garden room for relaxing and swimming. (Christian H. G. Wegener)

Who says a swimming pool has to be rectangular and use straight lines only? Jack Chandler, the great California garden designer, illustrates here how a swimming garden can take on a romantic and natural look—as long as sufficient space and financial means are both available.

120

Despite its simplicity, the effect here has not failed: two or three steps lead to the swimming pool, whose wall covering turns the water a striking dark blue. The nicely rustling grass relaxes the strict geometry of both the swimming pool and the patio under the pergola. (Jack Chandler & Associates)

In recent years, garden pools or basins have gone justly into disfavor. The reason: all too often, they have been placed in gardens tastelessly. Yet they provide a wonderfully stylish touch that can accent the appearance of a garden quite well. Of course, it is advisable to think in terms of traditionally tested balance and choose forms that please the eye. Square, rectangular, or round shapes offer—now as before—a wealth of formative possibilities. Experimenting in a formative sense should be avoided, as it offers only short-term success—if any. When searching for the best-suited form and materials for a water fountain, a look from the house into the garden is also worth taking. Architecture speaks a clear language, one that should be continued into the garden pool.

The Loveliest Garden Pools

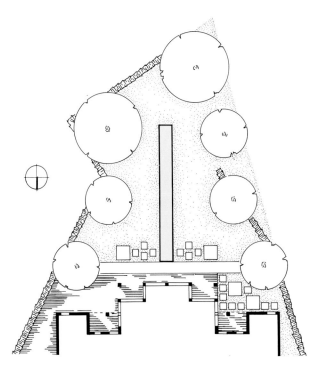

The plan: less can be more when it determines the garden architecture as strongly as in this garden. The long water table extends the central axis of the house into the garden, which is planted with individual shrubs only (Rheims & Partner). Scale: 1:400

A symmetrical, tastefully designed water table catches the eye in this garden. It also substitutes for a larger body of water, since the parents saw a planned pond as too dangerous for their children. The water table, a good forty-two feet long and almost five feet wide, consists of a black-painted steel body rising some sixteen inches above the grass. The water flows evenly over the rim, almost to the ground, and covers the steel structure like a tablecloth. At the bottom, the water is pumped back into circulation. (Rheims & Partner).

Left: The shallow pool, rimmed by a steel band and encircled by a narrow strip of greenery, forms a background for mobile art The three "quarter-spheres" of black granite (Max Bill) rise elegantly from the shallow water (Ivan Ruperti).

Right: Like a backbone, the concrete path picks up the symmetrical axis of the house and extends it through the garden, passing alongside the small pool to the patio of large basalt slabs (foreground). The regularity of the planting is broken by a another path, this one of granite slabs, that curves around the axis and borders the pool. A black and white shard mosaic adds additional interest. (Stephan Becsei).

A large round pool, white trellis, and inviting pavilion: everything is harmoniously combined and goes well together—almost as in a beautiful park (Gies).

Water and boxwood can successfully compete if laid out in geometrical shapes, as they are here. The boxwood beds cut at various heights join with the rectangular pools to offer new possibilities for garden architecture (Deroose).

Clear shapes and colors are often the best recipe for a garden's layout, such as this one on Ibiza. The narrow pool is designed very elegantly, with red slabs in the front and ground and a covering of green in the back.

Two long garden pools, set one after the other to form a long axis, display a stately elegance. Lady Florence Phillips planned this garden in her splendid residence not far from Capetown, South Africa.

How does one utilize the angular boundary of a piece of property? One way is with a water garden. This one consists of a small planted pool and a wooden footbridge leading to a white bench (A. Boesterling, Konstanz).

Fresh ground water flows from the lion's head into the walled spring of handmade bricks, creating a traditional piece of garden architecture on this property. From here, the water runs into the big swimming pond, which was made from a former swimming pool.

Still waters don't have to be deep. Here we see a clear, quiet surface between the mossy brick walls and paths, forming the center of a large patio (Groenewegen).

Right: This section of the "Harpers & Queen—Classic Garden" at the Chelsea Flower Show in London shows elements of eighteenth-century French garden culture that could also decorate present-day gardens. The shape of the arcade and the quiet of the water channel are classic, and thus timelessly beautiful (Clifton Landscape & Design).

The long boat looks as though it has run aground, with its bow a little higher out of the water. A close up view reveals that it is cast in concrete and rests on a frost-free foundation. The boat's walls are grooved on a large scale, ensuring the exchange of water between the concrete boat and the pond (Architect: Barnhard Hafner; Artist: Fedo Ertl, both of Graz).

Water, stones, and the green of grass and bamboo: this garden needs little else for interest. Above all, the water surface in the steel-rimmed pool gives the garden depth, provides an attractive contrast to the gravel, and mirrors the surroundings charmingly (Sven Kierkegaard).

Above and below: Symmetry is the theme of this garden area fronting a conservatory. Mirror-like and elegant, the two small pools extend before the glass structure with its ivy-covered pergolas and accompany the broad gravel walks to the patio. The pool rims are covered with lead—quite in the nice old tradition (Marcel Wolterinck).

This group of old yew trees, which the German landscape architect J. P. Posth planted some two hundred years ago at Huis Bingerden in Holland, grew into a beautiful garden "room," ideal for a quiet pool reflecting its surroundings of ivy and lady's mantle (S. E. van Weede).

The Best is the Water

The best models are provided by nature itself. There are many natural bodies of water in which the right position, the proportions, the variety of ecological niches, and the plants can all be observed. A puddle is the smallest natural body of water; with its meager depth, sunlight shines on its bottom. Standing waters are usually in naturally low or sunken places with impenetrable layers of clay. The quick warming of water in the spring encourages plants to grow and some amphibians to emerge. It is not unusual for the water to dry out completely in summer. A pond is a larger body of water, up to six feet of depth, in which plants grow from the bottom. And what we call lakes are large bodies of standing fresh water, most of which took form after the last ice age about fifteen thousand years ago. In their lightless depths, the water temperature is a constant forty degrees Fahrenheit. Brooks, lastly, should also be mentioned, as they allow observation of their flow and watercourse, windings, and shore-based plant life.

The Right Choice

The garden pond comes very close to simulating a natural pond: an artificial body of water with an average depth of two to four feet and a constant or regulated amount of water.

Natural Pond

When a natural pond has succeeded, it has the effect of a piece of pure nature in the midst of a garden. The banks, though created by human hands, resemble models in the world of nature with their soil, sand, and stones, and allow for planting of native plants in the swamp zone and shallow-water area. Fauna in the pond appear without any foreign influence: instead of goldfish, there are tadpoles and fish leeches, water beetles and insect larvae to enliven the pond water. Sometimes fish turn up as well, as sticky fish eggs stick to the feathers or legs of water birds such as ducks. When the birds visit the pond and enter the water, the eggs are loosened—it doesn't take long then till the first little fish can be seen.

Decorative Fish Pond

A pond with brightly colored goldfish is for many the very essence of a garden pond. But unlike a natural lake, in which carnivorous and vegetarian fish (those that eat water fleas, the filtrators of plant plankton) exist in a balanced relationship, the increase in fish population is difficult to control here. Through feeding, the water becomes too rich in nutrients and suffers more and more from lack of oxygen. It then becomes murky, resulting in the need for electric circulation and oxygenation pumps to ensure an adequate supply of oxygen. The population can be effectively limited by not feeding the fish or by adding pike.

Plans and Layouts

Details and Designs

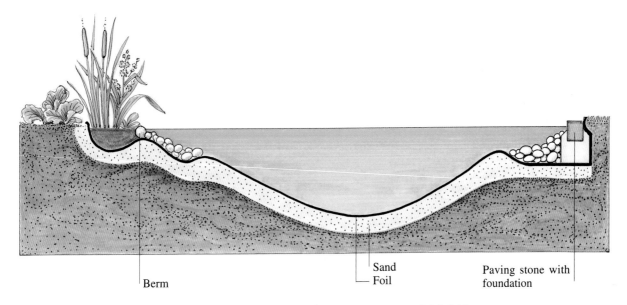

Berm

Sand
Foil

Paving stone with
foundation

This cross-section shows the right composi-
tion of a pond bottom. On the sides, the
ground is sloped with the help of berms and
deep spots are built. These are either covered
with gravel or filled with substrata and
planted. The pond bottom is covered with a
layer of sand, on which the pond foil is laid.
At left, the foil separates the pond area from
the dry shore zone. At right, the shoreline is
formed by a granite stone which is set in a
concrete support (detail of page 36).

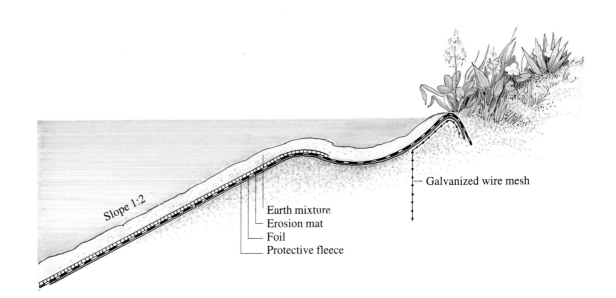

Slope 1:2

Galvanized wire mesh

Earth mixture
Erosion mat
Foil
Protective fleece

The water surface of this pond blends optically with the plants outside of it. A wire mesh
protects the pond foil from damage by moles.
The pond bottom consists of four layers: protective fleece, pond foil, an erosion-protection
mat and a layer, some eight inches thick, of
dug-out soil and a sand-gravel mix in equal
parts (detail of page 60).

139

Woodland Pond

A pond in the shade of trees can have its charm, with the sunlight shining softly through the treetops onto the water (see page 18). Of course, only a few plants survive in constant shade, where the water is scarcely warmed. In addition, the pond bottom will in time be covered by fallen leaves, unless this is prevented by using nets that are put up in autumn. When the water is not too cold, a varied slice of life develops on the pond shore; this includes amphibians such as frogs, turtles, and salamanders, as well as water beetles and such small fish as minnows.

Japanese Pond

In the Land of the Rising Sun, water is utilized as the most important basic element of garden formation. The quiet pond surface forms a contrast with the shore, strengthened with weighty stones, a brook or waterfall, small hills, or shaped shrubs and trees. This type of formation is also finding more and more fans in other areas (see pp. 20, 24, 30, 56, 68).

Swimming Ponds and Pools

For many garden owners, a swimming pool would be an expensive burden, one used too rarely to justify the high cost of energy for heating it. The usually rectangular swimming pool therefore becomes a foreign body in the garden. Why not turn it instead into a nearly natural swimming pond? The idea can be astounding: the walls are taken back some twenty inches, then the basin can be divided into various realms for the needs of miscellaneous water and swamp plants. To waterproof the bottom, pond foil with geofleece under it (to protect the foil from sharp angles) can be used. As the examples show (pp. 88-107), a swimming pond can cover several thousand square feet and have the look of a natural pond. The principle is really simple. First an unplanted swimming pool, about six feet deep, is set apart by concrete walls (like those of a rebuilt swimming pool) or an earthen wall under the water surface. The adjoining shallow shore area is planted for regeneration, and also used to warm the water.

Brook

To make a body of water in a garden livelier or to link two ponds together, a brook, sometimes in connection with a spring or waterfall, is an attractive element. On most properties, the prerequisites for it are right at hand. A slight difference in height on the lot is sufficient to provide for the necessary fall of at least one percent. Even where the ground is completely flat, one does not need to give up on a brook or a spring if the height difference can be created artificially with stones.

Moving, flowing water has very different forms of expression, which can be varied in an artificially created garden layout. The slope determines the flowing speed of the water. Brooks and rivers that move freely in the world of nature often have one-half percent of fall. In the garden, though, appearance is enhanced when the brook flows somewhat faster. Here, a fall of one to eight percent has proven itself.

The charm of a brook's course is in the change of its flowing speed, its width, its depth, and—don't forget—its plant life. Right after the spring, the water can flow through a narrow brook bed, then be dammed to make a small lake, and finally pour over a waterfall into the pond or continue on its way as a brook. Sometimes the shore is formed with gravel and bigger stones, sometimes swamp plants grow right up to the water. In large gardens, an appealing as well as very natural look can be achieved by having the brook flow through

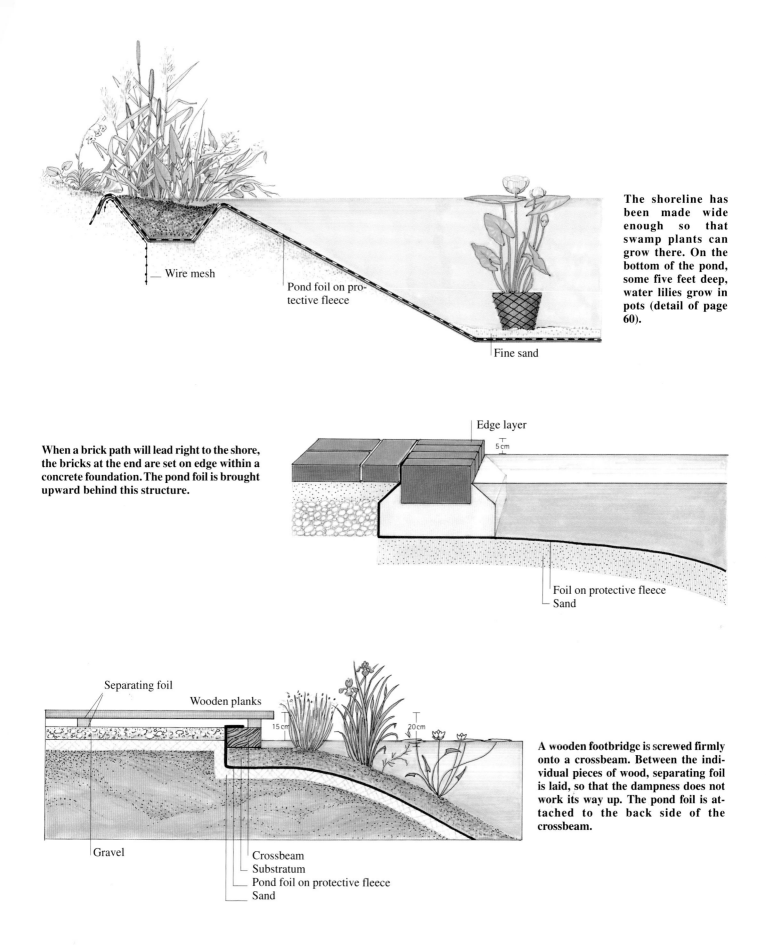

— Wire mesh

Pond foil on protective fleece

Fine sand

The shoreline has been made wide enough so that swamp plants can grow there. On the bottom of the pond, some five feet deep, water lilies grow in pots (detail of page 60).

When a brick path will lead right to the shore, the bricks at the end are set on edge within a concrete foundation. The pond foil is brought upward behind this structure.

Edge layer

5 cm

Foil on protective fleece
Sand

Separating foil
Wooden planks

15 cm

20 cm

Gravel

Crossbeam
Substratum
Pond foil on protective fleece
Sand

A wooden footbridge is screwed firmly onto a crossbeam. Between the individual pieces of wood, separating foil is laid, so that the dampness does not work its way up. The pond foil is attached to the back side of the crossbeam.

141

a flowering meadow, accompanied only by a few marsh marigolds or other flowers.

The depth of the brook bed should be only a few inches where the water is not dammed; some four to six inches are sufficient. Small stones can be laid in the brook's course so that they are partially visible above the water; this makes the surface look more interesting. For a small increase in water speed, the slope can be raised where the bed is made narrower and the sides flanked by large boulders. The flow takes on more speed when the water depth is reduced significantly here to two to four inches.

The Location

The question of location needs thorough consideration, as it involves fitting the pond both ecologically and architecturally into the garden layout. The advice of a garden architect is essential, so that the pond and brook will be included in the complete concept of the garden. It may seem obvious to place the pond directly by the terrace, but many owners prefer to see their nearly natural pond farther to the rear of the garden, to attract both the eye and the interest. Both positions have their virtues. More and more often, a big pond by the terrace, its large size comparable to the extent of lawn, wins out (see the row house garden, page 72). For swamp and water plants to bloom, sunshine is required, so a location that is in the sun for six to eight hours per day (during the summer months) should be selected. The great midday heat is not necessarily good for the plants, but will be appreciated by guests at the swimming pond. . . .

The Size

The more square feet of pond surface the better. A bigger pond will be gladly adopted by small animals and usually looks better, as it makes the garden seem more extensive and interesting. About three hundred square feet is an ideal size for many gardens, but no upper limits are set. The water of larger ponds undergoes much less temperature variation. The biological balance is established more quickly, and the relationship between open areas and planted areas is better balanced. When fish are desired, a depth of approximately three to four feet is dependable, although the whole pond does not have to be that deep. To provide a winter home for animals, a deep area about three feet in diameter on the pond bottom is sufficient. For a natural pond, the soil must be dug out to some thirty inches. For amphibians, on the other hand, a water depth of about six inches is enough.

The Shape

Anything is allowed, provided it fits into the overall scheme. Garden ponds are often laid out in free forms, the so-called kidney shape, with one part larger and deeper than the rest. This style, the shape of which is quickly overgrown and made invisible by plant growth, certainly has its advantages. Such ponds possess just what a garden pond needs: a large area of open water and a narrow, shallower part for the swamp plants. When geometrical forms dominate other aspects of a garden, a round or angular pond will fit in well. Combining several shapes, and perhaps linking them together by a narrow channel or brook, can also be optically attractive. Obviously, a pond with soft, natural shore zones fits into a garden more easily than a round, square, or rectangular shape, though the latter may look better beside the terrace of the house. And sometimes the planning of a garden calls for a clearly recognizable shape for the pond or garden pool.

The pond shore is firmed with rounded stones lying in a bed of mortar. The disadvantage of this is that the shore cannot be planted. The foil is brought upward behind the stones.

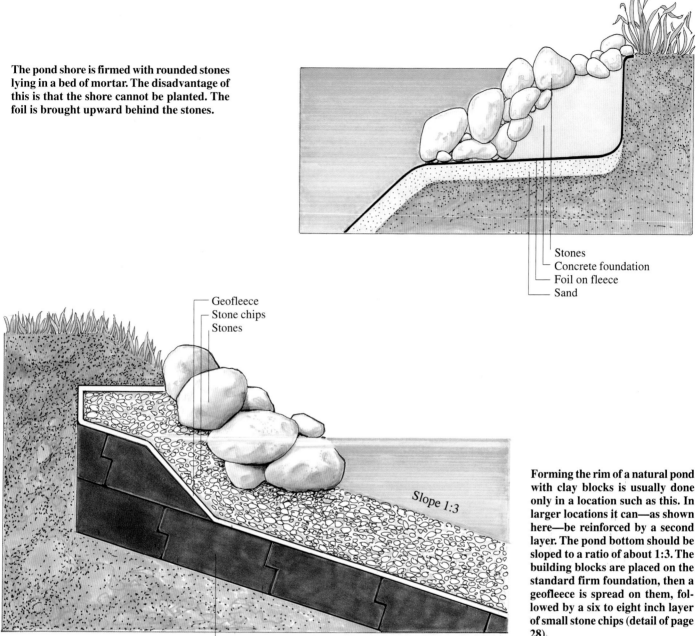

Stones
Concrete foundation
Foil on fleece
Sand

Geofleece
Stone chips
Stones

Slope 1:3

Clay building blocks

Forming the rim of a natural pond with clay blocks is usually done only in a location such as this. In larger locations it can—as shown here—be reinforced by a second layer. The pond bottom should be sloped to a ratio of about 1:3. The building blocks are placed on the standard firm foundation, then a geofleece is spread on them, followed by a six to eight inch layer of small stone chips (detail of page 28).

The Materials

Foil

Most water bodies have to be created artificially, with their bottoms protected against water loss. Various means of waterproofing can be considered. Most often, PVC pond foil is used, and for good reason: at this time there is no material that can be used more effectively. PVC, standing for Polyvinylchloride, is a byproduct of the processing of petroleum and cooking salt. This special pond foil is elastic, safe for fish, resistant to sour soil, frost, and corrosion, non-tearing, UV-stable, rot-free, root-secure—and very importantly—cadmium-free. It should have a thickness of at least one millimeter. It is best to have the foil prepared in the desired size. For a larger pond, a thickness of 1.5 millimeters is recommended.

On the other hand, the more expensive synthetic rubber foils (EPDM foils) are gaining popularity, as are the polyethylene (PE) foils, though they are firmer and form curves less well. Essentially, any foil that must be attached carefully to a smooth undersurface that is free of stones and jagged objects can be used (sand or geofleece can lie underneath it). This must particularly be considered when, for example, heavy boulders are to be placed on the foil in the shore zone.

Clay

It used to be customary to waterproof the bottom of a natural pond with clay, the so-called potter's clay. This is still possible today if one uses building elements made of clay. Here it is important to make the slope very gentle (maximum ratio 1:3). The four inch building blocks are laid on a geofilter fleece, overlapping, and tamped with a vibrating stamper. Finally, another fleece is laid on them, and a layer of chalk-free gravel, some eight inches thick, is added. This top layer prevents the clay from drying out, swelling too quickly, or being washed out.

Concrete

For large ponds, one often decides in favor of a stable layer of concrete. This requires a strong layer of frost protection (a gravel layer), on which a two inch layer of sprayed concrete is applied (using a special means of flowing). A grid of structural steel is laid on top to prevent cracking. Watertight concrete can also be used, though this usually makes watertight expansion joints necessary. Special asphalt concrete, a mixture of gravel, sand and bitumen, can also be used in two layers about two inches each, with a frost-protection layer added.

Polyester

Pools and ponds can be made watertight by covering their bottoms with polyester resin and fiberglass mats. This method is inexpensive but laborious, as several layers have to be placed on the bottom. Cracks in concrete basins can be repaired with this material.

The Pond Bottom

Special care must be devoted to the bottom of a pond, the area that determines what combination of plant and animal life will find a home in the artificial pond. As a rule of thumb, the pond surface should be ringed with a swamp zone twenty to forty inches wide. From there, the pond bottom can descend to its deepest point. A relationship of 1:2 (one vertical foot to two horizontal feet) or 1:3 is recommended. Vertical walls are a fatal trap for many animals.

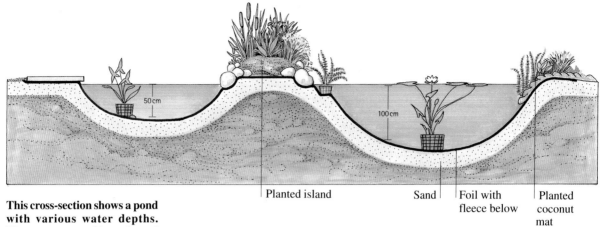

50 cm

100 cm

Planted island   Sand   Foil with   Planted
                                  fleece below   coconut
                                                mat

This cross-section shows a pond with various water depths. They are separated by a planted bed that rises above the water. In the same way, an island has been built in the pond.

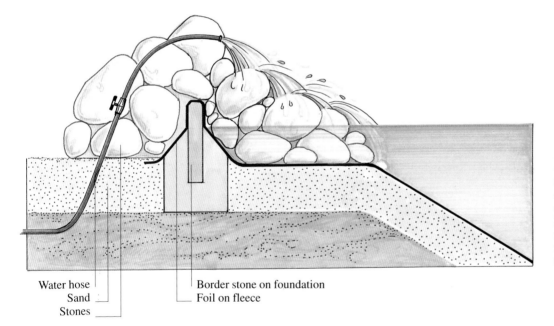

Water hose
Sand
Stones

Border stone on foundation
Foil on fleece

When an artificial spring is used to provide more life in a pond, the simplest way for it to emerge is from a pile of rounded stones. Here the pond shore is defined by border stone set on a concrete foundation. The hose, supplied with pond water from a circulation pump, is directed over this stone border (detail of page 76).

145

The Shore

The most beautiful yet most challenging jobs include forming the pond shores. As a rule, this usually visible zone should be made as a swamp zone, have a slight depth of water, and allow for natural transition to a dry zone of shrubs or grass. Here frogs and other amphibians will find an ideal spawning ground, and some of the loveliest flowers and grasses thrive in up to eight inches of water. Small stones and big boulders are not just a nice addition. They give the substrata of soil the necessary firmness, so that the soil does not slide or get washed away. The swamp zone should be at least twenty inches wide—a yard would be better. Between the wet zone at the shore and the dry land, a dividing zone should be set up. Otherwise, there is the danger of pond water being soaked up by the dry ground, which makes the water level in the pond sink remarkably fast.

A natural pond gets by without an entrance or exit. The excess water that comes into the pond from heavy rain is given off evenly to the shore. Even better, however, is when the water can flow from a spillway into an overflow trench. When water from the roof is directed into the pond through a brook, that water will enter the pond in a quite lovely way. Of course the water may be harmful: on the lee side of the roof, a coating of rust builds up if the house has oil heat. Mixing with rain water, it produces sulfuric acid, which then gets into the pond. This is often fatal for water animals.

The Substrata

Swamp and water plants need a sandy loam or clay bottom as a substratum and pond bottom. Sand alone would be sufficient, but it often does not give enough support to the taller flowers and reeds. Thus the loam content is important. The substrata should never be fertilized artificially, for nutrients hasten the development of algae. Those who plan to use available garden soil should make sure that it is nutrient-poor, like that dug out of the deepest area during the pond excavation. A mixture comprised of half this soil and half sand provides a good, economical substratum for both the pond bottom and the swamp zone at the shore.

The Water

Filling a pond gradually with rainwater is ideal, even though the water today is no longer pure and often very acid. Normally, however, the pond is filled with piped water. A favorable pH (acid) value is 7 to 8. In strong sunshine, the pH value increases. The water is not added in a hard stream, but in a spray. In this way, much less soil is washed away and a large part of the chlorine is already dissipated.

Safety

Where there is water, there is also danger for small children. They should never, therefore, be left unsupervised when in the vicinity of a body of water or able to find their way to it. A wide swamp zone, of course, lessens the danger, but not enough. When in doubt, install a fence at least two feet high to bar the way to the water. To ensure that small animals still have free access to the water, fences should clear the ground by some five inches. Special consideration must be given to small children when planning a pond for the front garden; homeowners may be required to remove a decorative pond if it could endanger small children from the neighborhood. When taking out liability insurance, it is advisable to include the dangers that a pond may cause. Finally, electric installations may be necessary for a pond, such as the power line for a circulation pump or light. This work belongs in the hands of a specialist!

A brook's course is waterproofed most simply with pond foil, which is laid on sand. Then comes a layer of mortar, in which the stones are embedded. The foil is raised behind the stone (see page 36).

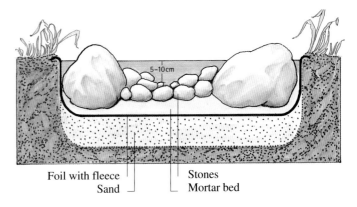

Foil with fleece
Sand
Stones
Mortar bed

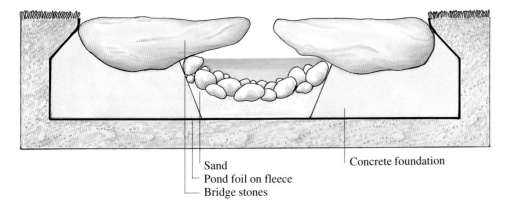

A bridge over a brook is made of two flat natural stones resting firmly on a concrete foundation. Between the "bridge stones," there is sufficient space for the water to flow through. Pond foil waterproofs the brook's course (see page 36).

Sand
Pond foil on fleece
Bridge stones
Concrete foundation

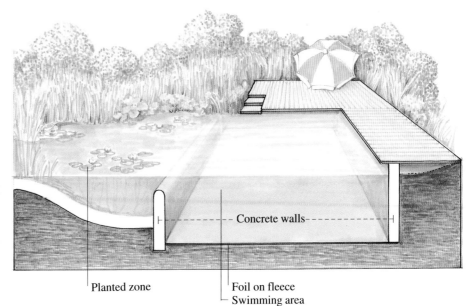

This shows the system used in "swimming ponds" (biosphere landscaping): the swimming area, with a depth of some six feet, is separated by a concrete wall from the shallow water zone, planted with reeds. To the right and back is a wooden platform with steps giving access to the water.

Planted zone
Foil on fleece
Swimming area
Concrete walls

147

Below: Water lilies: a must in most ponds and garden pools. As beautifully as they bloom, in this small pool it may soon be too crowded.

Right: Purple loosestrife (*Lythrum*) is one of the most grateful plants, as it blooms in both normal dry soil and in moist places for a long time. It also attracts many bees (Atelier für Landschaft und Garten).

Swamp and water plants are not just important to the appearance of a pond. Additionally, they are just as important to the pond's biological functioning as trees, grass, and shrubs are for a meadow or woodland glade. Originally land plants themselves, they have adapted to their changed surroundings in the course of their development.

The differences can be seen in the leaves and leaf stems. Unlike trees and shrubs, swamp and water plants have no firm tissue. Their stems do not become woody. Floating plants have special air chambers that keep the leaves on the surface of the water. The stems, often weakly formed, are intended less for carrying nutrients than for giving support in the ground.

Swamp and water plants—like land plants—produce oxygen (which the pond organisms vitally need), through daily photosynthesis. And they in turn keep the water clear. In addition, the pond plants reduce damaging nitrogen compounds in the water, and many even have a growth-inhibiting effect on the algae. The leaves of water plants offer countless small animals shelter from enemies, and many amphibians and fish use the greenery along the shore as a spawning ground. Some small animals even live in the stems. The caterpillar of one kind of butterfly lives and pupates in the stems of the cattails. When observing the plant life along a brook or pond, one can see that certain types have populated certain zones. Ponds, puddles, and lakes support different kinds of plant societies than do brooks. The quieter the water surface, the more numerous are its plants.

When planting a garden pond, it is best to start with natural or domesticated vegetation. Some varieties of plants, of course, have locations that cannot be limited clearly. Many plants thrive in both dry and moist soils. Noteworthy examples are purple loosestrife (*Lythrum salicaria*), pale yellow iris

The Plants

148

(*Iris pseudacorus*), marsh marigold (*Caltha palustris*) and water mint (*Mentha aquatica*).

The most important locations for plants at ponds and brooks can be divided into six areas:

Also On the Shore

This area is mainly occupied by "land plants." The soil has no connection with the water, but the location is influenced by the humid air near the water. Although any of the customary garden flowers could actually be planted here, only those that blend with the water plants in terms of their growth and appearance should be considered.

Some choices: bergenia (*Bergenia cordifolia*), spiderwort (*Tradescantia x andersoniana*), longleaf speedwell (*Veronica longifolia*), primrose (*Primula japonica*), lady's mantle (*Alchemilla mollis*), hosta (many *Hosta* types), Japanese iris (*Iris kaempferi*), largeleaf brunnera (*Brunnera macrophylla*), knotweed (*Polygonum affine, P. amplexicaule*), Siberian iris (*Iris sibirica*), day lily (*Hemerocallis*), and willowleaf sunflower (*Helianthus salicifolius*). Some grasses: Pacific Island silvergrass (*Miscanthus,* tall and short types), garden bamboo (*Fargesia murielae*), cordgrass (*Spartina*), and purple moorgrass (*Molinia caerulea*).

Marshy and Wet Ground

Plants in this realm are accustomed to continuous dampness, without the earth being covered with water (as would be typical of a swamp zone). Along a brook or at the edge of a garden pond such a realm can be created by widening the shore zone. The added soil should be higher than the water level, however. Most garden flowers will thrive in this zone, as will those that usually prefer the wetness of the swampy areas. Sometimes, such a moist area devel-

ops in a garden all by itself when surface water gathers in a low spot above loamy, impermeable soil. Even when the ground above dries out, the area remains wet enough for these plants: purple avens (*Geum rivale*), common comfrey (*Symphytum officinale*), narrow leaf blue-eyed grass (*Sisyrinchium angustifolium*), bird's-eye primrose (*Primula farinosa*), northern grass of Parnassus (*Parnassia palustris*), or devil's bite (*Succisa pratensis*). Sometimes this location will also be appreciated by colorful flowers such as purple loosestrife (*Lythrum salicaria*), large yellow loosestrife (*Lysimachia punctata*), quick-growing pestilence wort (*Petasites hybridus*), Indian rhubarb (*Peltiphyllum peltatum*), marsh marigold (*Caltha palustris*), swamp forget-me-not (*Myosotis palustris*), globeflower (*Trollius*), and hemp agrimony (*Eupatorium cannabinum*).

Swampy Areas

In water depths of six to eight inches, some of the loveliest plants thrive. This location offers two advantages. First, the choice is so great that one can omit "true" water plants and thus keep a sufficiently free water surface.

Top to bottom: blue-eyed grass (*Sisyrinchum angustifolium*) blooms in May and June. Marsh marigold (*Caltha*) is an early bloomer, often in March. Meadow bistort (*Polygonum bistorta "Superbum"*) should also be present.

Iris are important flowering plants by the water; in white, they almost seem to float in the air. Pampas grass (*Cortaderia*), often scorned as exotic, unfolds its charm when it blooms. Garden bamboo (recently named *Thamnocalamus spathaceus*) creates an evergreen coulisse.

In addition, this area is good for frog and salamander spawning. Swamp plants have to be capable of adapting to different water levels, as the level can sink significantly (especially from evaporation in summer). Some types will even survive a passing dry spell. The plants of this zone include: brook speedwell (*Veronica beccabunga*), water mint (*Mentha aquatica*), swordleaf rush (*Juncus ensifolius*), common buckbean (*Menyanthes trifoliata*), pontederia (*Pontederia cordata*), narrow leaf bur reed (*Sparganium emersum*), scouring rush horsetail (*Equisetum hyemale*), and zebra sedge (*Scirpus tabernaemontani "Zebrinus"*).

Shallow Water

At water depths up to twenty inches, plants with slim, upright growth thrive. The most important types are cattails, reeds, and pond rushes. With their long rhizomes, they hang onto the saturated bottom and grow very profusely. Within a short time, in fact, a single type of plant can dominate an area extending well into the middle of the pond.

Because of their thickly intertwined root systems in which the smallest bits of detritus or mud are held, the following plants (all of which are at home in this shallow-water zone) are preferred for planting in a swimming or swampy pond: broadleaf cattail (*Typha latifolia*), reed (*Phragmites communis*), sedge (*Scirpus lacustris*), and fluttering rush (*Juncus effusus*). These plants would not be at home along a brook, for they need still water. Also recommended for a garden pond are flowering rush (*Butomus*), water plantain (*Alisma plantago aquatica*), golden club (*Orontium aquaticum*), pontederia (*Pontederia cordata*), arrowhead (*Sagittaria sagittifolia*), and common mare's tail (*Hippuris vulgaris*).

1

2

3

4

5

6

150

Water Plants

Some of the most interesting plants thrive in areas where the water is more than twenty inches deep. They root in the pond bottom, and their leaves and blossoms float on the surface. Some root on the bottom without coming to the surface; others float freely in the water. The European white water lily (*Nymphaea alba*), on which many new breeds are based, is one of the most beautiful plants of this zone. Also lovely are the yellow pond lily (*Nuphar lutea*), the floating pondweed (*Potamogeton natans*), the yellow floating hearts (*Nymphoides peltata*), the cape pondweed (*Aponogeton distachyos*), or water knotweed (*Polygonum amphibium*). Among the floating water plants are the frogbit (*Hydrocharis morsus-ranae*), water soldiers (*Stratiotes aloides*), eared watermoss (*Salvinia natans*), giant duckweed (*Spirodela polyrhiza*), and water chestnut (*Trapa natans*).

Underwater Plants

These plants do not appear at all—or only in passing—on the water surface. For pond water they are indispensable. They produce much oxygen and also give off nutrients into the water, thus preventing algae growth. Many spread quickly, however, and can become a nuisance: the water may certainly be clear, but is too full of plants— an indication that the plants should be thinned out now and then.

Underwater plants have varying requirements, thus not every kind thrives well in a pond. The preferred water depth is between eight and thirty-two inches. Some of the most important plants are: Coon's tail (*Ceratophyllum demersum*), curly pondweed (*Potamogeton crispus*), needle spikerush (*Eleocharis acicularis*), spike water milfoil (*Myriophyllum spicatum*), and waterweed (*Elodea canadensis*).

The blue of the iris flowers is increased by their reflection in the water.
The gunnera (*Gunnera*) needs fertilizer for the leaves to become really luxurious.
Two lovely flowers that blossom in late summer: knotweed (*Polygonum amplexicaule*) and hemp agrimony (*Eupatorium*).

Spring gets off to a good start with these bergenia flowers.
The edge of the pond: surrounded by lady's mantle (*Alchemilla*), not only beautiful at blossoming time.
Water buttercup (*Ranunculus aquatica*) should clean the water, and it spreads quickly and decoratively.

Below: Ducks on a visit to the pond, but an unmatched pair; one was obviously fooled by the sight of the other. As lovely as ducks may be, in ponds they disturb the plants along the shore.

Before the decision is made to stock fish or not—and what kind—vigorous life and activity will already be going on in the pond. Take the trouble to observe the water quietly from a "frog's-eye view": water striders, various types of water beetles, dragonflies, water bugs, and scorpions will be the first to settle at the pond. Along with the newly planted swamp and water plants, algae, bacteria, worms, and small crustaceans will appear. A garden pond will be enriched with little animals more quickly when it is "inoculated" with water from another, more "natural" body of water (one or two buckets are usually enough).

If the surroundings of the pond offer protection and shade, it will not be long before amphibians arrive: turtles and frogs, newts, and salamanders. All will show up and remain by an artificial body of water in a garden if the conditions are favorable. Amphibians include all those vertebrates that live in two different regions: both the water and the land. The animals, of course, are created in the water and developed there as larvae. As adults, they also live outside the water.

Among the unexpected inhabitants of a garden pond are snails—especially those that live on algae, although they also consume plant parts and dead animals. In oxygen-poor water it is easy to see these snails move along the surface of the pond and audibly inhale oxygen. For life in a garden pond, fresh-water mussels can also be important. They filter the water and are also needed by carp for spawning. The mussels, usually obtained from fish-growing firms, are set in a bowl-shaped, sandy place on the bottom of the pond.

For many garden owners, however, a pond remains incomplete without fish; they miss the visible, moving life in the water. Unfortunately, only with a small "trick" is it possible for fish and frogs to reproduce jointly in a pond. Those who would like stocked fish as well as natural pond life should protect the frog eggs from the fish with a screen. Every decorative fish pond is really an intrusion into the natural food chain. Fish live on amphibian and insect larvae, insects, and other small animals. In a garden pond, however, the natural urge to eat that exists in large lakes is lacking. Decorative fish have no enemies here and can reproduce as they please. The result can be misery if the fish growth is not kept under control and additional oxygen not provided.

Animal Life in and on the Water

As more and more garden owners become aware of nature and the environment, interest in native fish is increasing—although their camouflage colors are not as attractive those of exotic fish. The same is true of these fish as of their exotic counterparts, however: they really don't belong in a body of water where they can multiply too fast for lack of enemies. Exceptions prove the rule: some of the young carp will be eaten by beetle and dragonfly larvae, which regulates their numbers naturally. Carp only multiply when the freshwater mussels they need for spawning are present; the males in particular are attracted by bright colors at spawning time.

The roach and redeye are also nice school fish, about eight inches long. They eat insects and larvae, as well as vegetable matter such as the leaves of swamp and water plants. Minnows, a small carp type, are about six inches long. They also live on small water insects. A school of minnows, though, should only be turned loose in a pond when sufficient quantities of oxygen can be supplied.

Crustaceans are another charming addition to a pond. Don't worry about them nipping your toe if you are standing on the shore or swimming in the water. Crabs, which are only active at night, won't harm any warm-blooded creature, nor will they attack goldfish, Koi, or birds. These crabs, native for millions of years (and not to be confused with Turkish crabs which, like other imported crabs, carry deadly diseases), have a stiff outer shell. Their flexible body parts are linked by thin, firm, clear skin. Their "armor" cannot grow with them, therefore the crab "molts" when its body weight increases. In a few days their new white skin hardens. These "water policeman" live on removable plant parts and water insects. From their fourth year on, they do not reject dead fish or frogs.

Crabs live in colonies of at least ten individuals. Twelve square yards of water surface in a pond that does not completely freeze in the winter is the minimum. Larger ponds are better, as then the crabs do not need to be fed extra. They reproduce quite fast, and from a weight of about three ounces up, can be eaten as a delicacy. Special traps, with a fresh piece of fish as bait, are used to catch them.

Above: Crabs should not be lacking in a big pond, as these "water policeman" keep the water clean. And don't fear their claws: they look more dangerous than they are.

Left: The loveliest, most shimmering, and most expensive goldfish are the Koi, a Japanese carp species. A blend of red, black, silver, and gold gives the fish its charm. Koi do not belong in a natural pond, where they would soon become invisible (since carp feed in bottom mud and muddy the water). At a depth of five feet they can spend the winter outside.

153

Spring Maintenance

When root pieces of water plants such as water lilies rot, they should be cut off and put in compost. This must be done carefully, though, for frogs and turtles will come to spawn when the first plants appear and the marsh marigolds bloom. New water plants should be planted as of around May, when the water is already warm.

Summer Maintenance

Swamp and water plants can be handled at any time. If floating or underwater plants have spread out too much, some of them can be removed. Electric circulation pumps, if being used, should be checked periodically to be sure the intake is free and not clogged. If fish are stocked in the pond, feed them sparingly. Only special food, spread on a water surface of ten to thirty square feet, should be used; this will allow all the fish to get some of it. Fish should only be fed when the water is at least 50 to 60 degrees Fahrenheit. With normal plant growth, goldfish can get along without extra food, do not grow as much, and scarcely multiply.

What To Do About Algae

On warm, sunny days in early summer, when the water on the pond surface is warm, algae quickly take over. A pond full of nutrients will get particularly dull and begin to "bloom," as the algae gain from the nutrients in the water. Under these conditions, the underwater plants in the cooler and deeper levels of the pond cannot compete. Small crabs, water fleas, and other small animals that consume algae are not yet active. The result: all day the algae produce oxygen, which they consume at night. The pond water can then become unbalanced. With increased warming of the water, small

Maintenance

life forms end their hibernation state and wiggle out of their eggs. In a few days the plant plankton—the algae—will get eaten up, and the water will be clear. But if nutrients become meager again, many water fleas will die. As they rot, nutrients become free and the water can turn murky again. In a well-planted pond, swamp plants provide a balance by using up the nutrients from the water and the ground. In a new or insufficiently planted pond, the water will become murky at first no matter what.

There are many kinds of algae. *Gravel algae* feel slightly rough. They cause a transitory greenish tinge to the water in the spring. *Blue algae* live on the surface in large colonies. In new ponds they form the "water blooming" effect. With a very rich supply of nutrients and high water temperatures, *stringy blue algae* can be seen forming thick, musty-smelling bubbles on the surface. *Thread algae* should be tolerated if they appear in small numbers. They bind excess nutrients and make the pond water look clear. If they become too numerous, fish some of them out. Although it may be tempting to use a "chemical club" (in the form of algae poison), this is no way to make the water in the pond clear and the algae will just grow all over again. Effective measures are:

- using nutrient-poor pond soil and—best of all—gravel
- "neutralizing" calcium-rich water with rainwater or white turf
- feeding the fish less or not at all
- planting a variety of plants on the shore
- planting underwater plants like horn wort (*Ceratophyllum*), water milfoil (*Myriophyllum*), water star wort

(*Callitriche*), and spikerush (*Eleocharis*). They produce oxygen and are important as hiding and resting places for pond life.

Replacing the murky pond water does not bring improvement, for fresh tap water contains no fewer nutrients and the algae will reproduce faster than before. There is a new product called Aquatop that improves the water quality and slows down algae growth.

Can Water Plants Be Reduced?

Duckweed includes the smallest blooming plants, consisting of a floating part and usually short roots. In heavily fertilized standing water they indicate a high percentage of nitrogen. They increase very quickly (as can be seen in many canals in Holland). Their thick growth on the pond surface prevents light from reaching the lower levels and reduces the gas exchange between water and air. As a result, inert gases build up and the pond water becomes unbalanced. These plants should be taken out with a net. Grass carp also reduce them—as well as algae—permanently.

Maintenance in Autumn

Every leaf from the surrounding trees, shrubs, and swamp plants that gets into the pond water is a biological mass. Gradually, a layer of mulch builds up on the pond bottom. Over time this turns to mud, which gives off inert gases—thus oxygen is consumed. To slow this development, it is advisable to spread a net when leaves are falling, keeping as many leaves as possible out of the pond in the first place. Since the pond creatures prepare for winter during the autumn, extreme movement of the water should be avoided. Fish should spend the winter only when the pond is deeper than thirty inches.

If an electric circulation pump is in use as a water filter or "spring," it should be removed before a heavy frost and stored frost-free in a container filled with water. Those who want to can also run the pump in winter. At temperatures below freezing, interesting "icebergs" will arise from the freezing water. Be sure the pump always has a sufficient supply of water, as it will become defective if it dries out.

The frequency with which a pond must be cleaned depends on the height of the rotting level on its bottom and the water quality. Cleaning can be necessary after only three years, or it can take more than ten years until the water must be partly or wholly removed and the bottom layer removed. All the plants from the pond can be composted.

Maintenance in Winter

A pond can be used for ice skating when a strong layer of ice has built up. If fish are under the ice, it should not be stepped on, however. Fish react very strongly to sound. They must also be sup-

plied with oxygen. With enough shore planting, adequate oxygen usually gets into the water via the plant stems. One can also put in a bundle of fresh straw or the like vertically. In any case, the layer of ice should not enclose the entire surface of the pond.

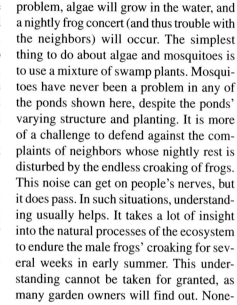

Now and then mosquitoes become a problem, algae will grow in the water, and a nightly frog concert (and thus trouble with the neighbors) will occur. The simplest thing to do about algae and mosquitoes is to use a mixture of swamp plants. Mosquitoes have never been a problem in any of the ponds shown here, despite the ponds' varying structure and planting. It is more of a challenge to defend against the complaints of neighbors whose nightly rest is disturbed by the endless croaking of frogs. This noise can get on people's nerves, but it does pass. In such situations, understanding usually helps. It takes a lot of insight into the natural processes of the ecosystem to endure the male frogs' croaking for several weeks in early summer. This understanding cannot be taken for granted, as many garden owners will find out. Nonetheless, no one should be deprived of his or her property—be it a swampy meadow, natural pond, or brook—when it can be avoided, for each of us gains from a garden pond. Certainly the environment gains, and we are a part of it.

Appendix

Garden and Landscape Architects and Planners

Anderson-Schwartz Architects
180 Varick Street
New York, New York 10014
pp. 112, 113

Architektbüro Landschaft + Garten
Jürgen Papenfuss, Jürgen Rösner
Oelmuehle
42699 Solingen, Germany
pp. 60-63, 80, 81, 149

Bambek + Bambek
Architektur + Design
Strümpfelbacher Strasse 58A
70327 Stuttgart, Germany
pp. 64, 65

Stephan Becesi
Raimundstrasse 7
60431 Frankfurt, Germany
p. 127

Siegmund Behr
Garten- und Landschaftsarchitekt
BDLA
Sattelhofweg 2A
29227 Celle, Germany
pp. 76, 77

Dick Beyers
Studio voor Tuinkunst
Konigin Wilhelmina Laan 18
NL-2012 Haarlem, Netherlands
p. 9

Biotop Landschaftsgestaltung
GmbH
Hauptstrasse 285
A-3411 Weidling, Austria
title page, pp. 89-91, 102, 103

Bödeker, Boyer
Wagenfeld & Partner
Landschaftsarchitekten BDLA
Bergische Landstrasse 606
40629 Düsseldorf, Germany
pp. 52-55.

Jack Chandler & Associates
Landscape Architects
PO Box 2180
Yountville, California 94599
pp. 5, 108-111, 114-117, 120, 121

Clifton Landscape & Design
5a Clifton Villas, Little Venice
London W9 2PH, Great Britain
p. 135

Paul Deroose
Stationstraat 166
B-1220 Jabbeke, Belgium
p. 129

Leo and Lydia Groenewegen
Hoker Stadtweg 1
NL-5835 CJ Beugen
Netherlands
pp. 134, 151

Grün plan
Planungsgruppe für Landschafts-
planung
und Gartenarchitektur
Oberstrasse 13A
30167 Hannover, Germany
pp. 28, 29

Beate Hodja
Garten- und Landschaftsarchitektin
Neelandstieg 7
21147 Hamburg, Germany
pp. 18, 19

Amy van Ierssel
De Rhulenhof
Kleefse Wej 14
NL-6595 NN Ottersum, Nether-
lands
p. 8

Inspired by Nature
Auenstrasse 78
80469 Munich, Germany
pp. 68-71, 94, 95

Angelika Kern, Albin Gilma
Seerosen Kern
Einödhofweg 20
A-8042 Graz, Austria
pp. 92, 93, 100, 101, 104, 105

Planungsbüro für Landschafts- und
Gartenstaltung
Horst Köhler
Auf dem Kamp 24
47800 Krefeld, Germany
pp. 106, 107

Knut Lehrke
Garten- und Landschaftsarchitekt
Quellenweg 2
53639 Königswinter, Germany
pp. 15-17

Wolf-Eckart Lüps
Architekt BDA
(with Peter Mengele)
Waldaweg 2
86919 Utting, Germany
pp. 40, 41

Michael Müller
(P. Harms & M. Müller
Garten- und Landschaftsbau)
Kiefernstrasse 1
49565 Bramsche, Germany
pp. 96-99

Wolfgang R. Mueller + Partner
Landschafts- und Gartenarchitekt
BDLA
Siemensring 106
47877 Willich, Germany
pp. 74, 75

Peter Neuberger
Landschaftsarchitekt BDLA
Senserbergstraße 21
82256 Fürstenfeldbruck, Germany
pp. 78, 79

Wolfgang H. Niemeyer
Landschaftsarchitekt BDLA
Stöberlstrasse 27
80687 Munich, Germany
pp. 40, 41

Dr. Willem Overmars
de Warande
Jan de Jagerlaan 2
NL-6998 AN Laag Keppel, Netherlands
p. 149

Corrie Poley-Bom and
Joop Poley
Dorpsplein 25
NL-Nisse/Zeeland, Netherlands
p. 2

Volker & Helgard Püschel
Freie Landschaftsarchitekten
BDLA
Wollenhausweg 5
40822 Mettmann, Germany
pp. 66-67

Rheims & Partner
Landschafts- und Garten-
architekten BDLA
Uerdinger Strasse 321
47800 Krefeld, Germany
pp. 72, 73, 124, 125

Studio Renate Richi
Sydikum 3
38108 Braunschweig, Germany
pp. 20-23

Roji Japanische Gärten
Reiner & Gesine Jochems
Alt-Moabit 49
10555 Berlin, Germany
pp. 55-56

Klaus Rudloff
Dipl.-Ing. Architekt
Parallelstrasse 12A
22851 Norderstedt, Germany
pp. 82, 83

Dr. Ivan Ruperti
Casa Maria
CH-6974 Aldesago-Lugano, Switzerland
pp. 50, 51, 126

Spengler Wiescholek
Freie Architekten
Stauffenbergstrasse 1
22587 Hamburg, Germany
pp. 18, 19

Bibliography

Manufacturers and Dealers

Team Grün-Plan
Konrad Wittich & Partner
Fasanenweg 9
61273 Wehrheim, Germany
pp. 84-87

Ulrich & Hannelore Timm
Grünplanung
Papenhuder Strasse 40
22087 Hamburg, Germany
pp. 30-33, 123

S. E. van Weede
Huis Bingerden
Bingerdenseweg 21
NL-6986 CE Angerlo, Netherlands
p. 137

Christian H. G. Wegener
Garten- und Landschafts-
architekt BDLA
Quellental 12+15
22609 Hamburg, Germany
pp. 36-39, 42-45, 120

Henk Weijers Gardens BV
Lorentzplein 15
NL-2012 HG Haarlem, Netherlands
pp. 34, 35, 46-49

Marcel Wolterinck B.V.
Naarderstraat 12
NL-1251 AW Laren, Netherlands
p. 136

Allison, James
Water in the Garden
London 1991

Baensch, Hans A.
Gartenteich-Atlas
Melle 1992

Bruns, Annelore, & Susanne
Hubert
Biogarten Praxisbuch
Munich 1987

Croutier, Alev Lytle
Wasser—Elixier des Lebens
Munich 1992

Durrer, Heinz
Wir beobachten am Weiher
Basel 1984

Hendel, Hubert
Wasser im Garten
Niedernhausen 1986

Ludwig, Herbert W.
Erlebnis Gartenteich
Munich 1992

Schimana, Walter, Cornelia Bott,
Lisa Bott-Bächle
Der Kosmos Ideengeber
Wassergärten
Stuttgart 1990

Steinbach, Günter (ed.)
Werkbuch Naturschutz
Stuttgart 1988

Swindells, Philip
Water Gardening
London 1994

Thielcke, Gerhard (et al.)
Rettet die Frösche
Stuttgart 1983

Wachter, Karl
Der Wassergarten
Stuttgart 1993

WDR-Gartenbuch
Es grünt so grün
Cologne 1994

Aguaplan
Held GmbH
Postfach 24
75050 Gemmingen, Germany
(PE foils)

Dia-Teichbauelemente
H. Dieckmann
31275 Lehrte, Germany
pp. 28, 56

Edelkrebszucht
Theo Grabowski
Annabergstrasse 2
86470 Thannhausen, Germany
p. 153

Österreichische Aquatop
Karl Sailer
Untermühlham 15
A-4891 Pöndorf, Austria

Re-Natur GmbH
Charles-Ross-Weg 24
24601 Ruhwinkel, Germany
(Headquarters with many branches)
Pond foil (also for swimming
ponds), water plants, etc.

Vosschemie
Esinger Steinweg 50
25436 Utersen, Germany
p. 30 (polyester)

Photo Credits

1	Peter Munster
2	Gary Rogers
4, 5	Gary Rogers
6	Jürgen Becker
7	Gary Rogers
8-11	Jürgen Becker
12, 13	Gary Rogers
15-17	Gary Rogers
18, 19	Horst Thanhäuser
20-23	Gary Rogers
25-27	Marion Nickig
28, 29	Grün plan archives
30-33	Gary Rogers
34	Peter Munster
35	Gary Rogers
37-39	Wolfram Stehling
40, 41	Wolfgang Niemeyer archives
42-45	Wolfram Stehling
46-49	H. Weijers Garden
50, 51	Gary Rogers
52, 53	Hajo Willig
54, 55	Jürgen Becker
56-59	Roji archives
61-63	Gary Rogers
64-65	Bambek + Bambek archives/R. Schenkirz
66, 67	Jürgen Becker
68-71	Sammy Hart
72, 73	Rheims & Partner archives
74, 75	Jürgen Becker
76, 77	Gary Rogers
78, 79	Birgit Amend/Burda Syndication
80, 81	Marion Nickig
82, 83	Dieter Steffen
85, 86	Konrad Wittich (86 top, center)
86, 87	Lars Kraume (86 bottom)
89-91	Biotop Landschaftsgestaltung archives
92, 93	Peter Munster
94, 95	Inspired by Nature archives
97	Peter Munster
98, 99	Felix Borkenau
100	Peter Munster
101	Seerosen Kern archives
103	Biotop Landschaftsgestaltung archives
105	Peter Munster (top)
105	Seerosen Kern archives (bottom)
107	Planungsbüro H. Köhler archives/W. zur Hausen
109-113	Gary Rogers
114-117	Andrew McKinney
118	Gary Rogers
119	Daniel & Emmanuelle Minassian
120	Gary Rogers (top, center)
120	Jennifer Chandler (bottom)
121	Andrew McKinney
123	Peter Munster
124-125	Carola Kohler/Rheims & Partner archives
126	Gary Rogers
127	Jens Willebrand/Schöner Wohnen
128	Gary Rogers
129	Jürgen Becker
130	Gary Rogers
131	Peter Munster
132	Jürgen Becker
133	Gary Rogers
134	Marion Nickig (top)
134	Peter Munster (center)
134	Horst Thanhäuser/Häuser (bottom)
135	Gary Rogers
136	Peter Munster
137	Jürgen Becker
148-149	Jürgen Becker
150	Peter Munster (5), Gary Rogers (1)
151	Peter Munster (4), Marion Nickig (1), Gary Rogers (1)
152	Peter Munster
153	Gary Rogers (top)
153	Michael Müller (bottom)
154	Jürgen Becker
155-156	Gary Rogers
158-159	Gary Rogers

Acknowledgments

To all architectural bureaus and their staffs, to the property owners, firms, and photographers, hearty thanks for their pleasant participation. In particular, thanks to the architect Markus Lampe, who put all the ground plans into a unified graphic form, and to Bärbel Bratge for the cutaway drawings. Without the generous cooperation of all those involved, this book would not have been possible.

Text editing:
Hans-Joachim Györffy.

Translated from the German by Ed Force

Library of Congress Cataloging-in-Publication Data

Timm, Ulrich.
Creating ponds, brooks, and pools: water in the garden / Ulrich Timm; with the cooperation of Hannelore Timm.
  p. cm.
ISBN: 0-7643-0915-3
1. Water gardens. 2. Water in landscape architecture. I. Title.
SB423.T56 1999
714--dc21   99-14408
                                                                              CIP

Printed in China.
ISBN: 0-7643-0915-3

This book was originally published under the title,
Die Neuen Teiche, Bäche, Pools
by Callwey

We are interested in hearing from authors with book ideas on related topics.